Shattering the Icons

FRANK M. LUNA

Copyright © 2016 Frank M. Luna
All rights reserved
First Edition

PAGE PUBLISHING, INC.
New York, NY

First originally published by Page Publishing, Inc. 2016

ISBN 978-1-68289-957-1 (pbk)
ISBN 978-1-68289-958-8 (digital)

Printed in the United States of America

Contents

Part I:
Abuelita's Farm: Cows, Chickens, and Culture

Chapter 1: Rise and Shine, *Cabrones*! 13
Chapter 2: The Udder Imbroglio of a Cow Hand 15
Chapter 3: What to Seize First, the Chicken or the Egg? 19
Chapter 4: You Say, "Peenso," I Say, "Pencil," Let's
Call the Whole Thing off 22
Chapter 5: From Commie to Cocoanut: My Betrayal
to *La Raza* 25

Part II: Fresno State University:
From Indoctrination to Revelation

Chapter 6: Histrionics in Bob's Class: I Scream, You
Scream, We All Scream for Ice Cream 31
Chapter 7: Social and Racial Inequality in Beth's
Class: Scrub that Tub, Mammy, and
Don't Forget to Call me Ma'am 35
Chapter 8: Soviet Communism: Working Men of all
Countries Unite, You Have Nothing to
Lose but Your Lives! Discovery and Revelation 39
Chapter 9: Soviet Communism: Working Men of All
Countries Unite, You Have Nothing to
Lose but Your Lives! The Gulag 43

Chapter 10: Soviet Union: Collectivization,
           Starvation, and Its Marxist Brood.............46
Chapter 11: The Purified Cesar Chavez and the
           United Farmworkers' Movement:
           Canonized and Cropped for his Beatification...........64
Chapter 12: Let's Just Say we turn the Other Cheek:
           The Ufw, Cesar Chavez, and a Messianic Complex ..71
Chapter 13: American Leftist Professorial Hypocrisy:
           "I Am A Marxist"—But I Would Rather
           Enjoy Life In The Capitalist US................76

Part III:
My Students: The Good, the Bad, and the Not-So-Pretty

Chapter 14: Critical Thinking in the Classroom: To
           Bomb or Not to Bomb, That is the Question...........91
Chapter 15: In Country: Bill and Patrick's Not-So-
           Excellent Combat Adventures in Vietnam.............103
Chapter 16: Judy's Blues: "I Don't Have the Time to
           Work in Your Class, But You *Still* Have to
           Pass Me, Mr. Luna!"................................110
Chapter 17: The Forgettable Instructor: I Remember
           Pete, but Pete Doesn't Remember Me................113
Chapter 18: From Gangsta with a Glock to Guru: The
           Story of Raj.......................................123
Chapter 19: Be Chary of Chatting with Your Chonies
           Down: The Trials and Tribulations of Technology ..132

Part IV: Afterthoughts

Chapter 20: Picking Up the Pieces: Reflections on the
           Shattered Icons....................................147

Acknowledgements

I would like to thank Dallas Wilcox, Trevor Boyd, and Stephen Matthews at Page Publishing for their guidance in this book. I wish to extend my deepest gratitude to Dr. Alfred J. Claassen, Dr. Robin Higham, and Dr. Sidney H. Chang for their instruction. Also, posthumously, I thank Dr. David N. Jones, Dr. Loy Bilderback, Dr. Jesus Luna, and Dr. John W. Bohnstedt. Finally, I am indebted to my wife, Tamie Yasukawa Luna, for her patience in allowing me to complete this work.

Some student names have been changed to protect their identity.

Introduction

A dark dictatorial Marxist cloud has descended upon the collegiate academic world in the United States of America. Beginning with the Bolshevik Revolution in Russia in 1917, its pathologic ideology eventually spread to enslave a third of mankind. Seemingly discredited with the fall of the Soviet Union in 1991, its doctrine still continues in a handful of oppressive nations—but just as alarming, and perhaps ironically, it has found a thriving and lucrative haven in the United States today. Streaming to the United States in the 1930s and flourishing in the 1960s and 1970s, it continues in colleges and universities that proclaim themselves to be institutions of diversity but are in fact institutions of indoctrination. This intellectual bias has effectively expunged divergent points of view and has thus made the college classroom a center for partisanship rather than education. This myopia of thought that is found mostly in academics trained in the social sciences and humanities has propagated in the minds of these instructors and today, through their succeeding academic progeny, has now reached frightening dimensions. A 2007 report by two liberal academics noted that Leftist professors in the United States outnumber conservatives in the social sciences and humanities by a frightening ratio of nine to one.[1] Buttressed by a mostly sycophantic media, generations of college instructors have seen themselves not only as educators but also as agents of social change. Many of the recent generations of academics are the intellectual products of the 1960s and 1970s, immersed in the cataclysm of the social upheavals of the times: the Vietnam War, racism, classism, feminism, the farmworker's movement, and more. Forged from these cultural fires arose a new Phoenix, academics anointed in the holiness of their cause. And as fire-breathing missionaries, these individuals found their task in the classroom not to teach but rather to indoctrinate new disciples for the cause.

Eschewing conventional religion, these propagators ironically adhere to a new faith, the salvation to the suffering of the world, and that is Marxism, heretofore referred to in its various incarnations: Communism, Socialism, the Old Left, the New Left, and Progressivism. Although there are variants within these classifications that differ, the vital core remains the same: a revolution of global dimensions that will eradicate the ills of the world—namely capitalism and its attendant institutions—and usher in a heaven-on-earth utopia. And like any faith, there must be good and evil. Good is the new world yet to come as prognosticated by founder Karl Marx: a classless society where the current inequalities of wealth will be swept away, and all will share equally in the bounties of the earth. Evil is Capitalism, that damnable institution that produces class distinctions by the enslavement of the masses to nefarious working conditions and wage slavery. But these new generations of believers did not see in their ideology a faith—no, that was for the unenlightened; rather, these new generations of instructors insisted their doctrine is science based on fact. Consequently, their task was and still is to propagate this new science as an inevitable fact; a new era that is going to cleanse the global soul of the evil that is Capitalism and prepare young minds for what is to come: an unending era of justice and equality where the oppressed are oppressed no more.

SHATTERING THE ICONS

I too was once a Marxist disciple. Raised in the latter half of the tempestuous '60s and '70s and ideologically indoctrinated by my very liberal mother and grandmother, I had no doubt about the cause. Buttressed by the media and the academic world, seemingly everyone was in concurrence about what the problem was and what needed to be done. So as I grew and even through high school, I continued to be a fervent devotee, certain of my convictions.

This certainty continued with my matriculation at Fresno State University, and most of the instructors I encountered were also of a like mind. Yet as will be noted below, it was there that I began to question my once unshakable beliefs. After a couple of years, I began to notice a teaching methodology employed by many of my professors. I noticed, sometimes in an overt and other times in a subtle way, the way in which my Leftist instructors manipulated their students and the information they presented in class. I also observed legitimate student queries dismissed, and I realized the materials and topics professors raised in class were biased. Also, some countries and institutions that these professors slavishly idolized globally, (e.g., Communist states, and locally [e.g., the United Farm Workers Movement (UFW)]), should also be accepted unquestioningly by their students as advocates for the poor and oppressed. Agitated by this bias, I began an intensive inquiry of my own to investigate this accepted academic dogma. And at the conclusion of my perusal, I discovered that these assertions by my professors were false. These countries and institutions, purported to be advocates for the downtrodden, were exactly the opposite; they were just another form of oppression against the very people they claimed to help.

I also discovered that the elite members of these movements lived separately and lavishly apart from the masses, in the same manner that Marxist professors in the United States detached themselves from American society. Although the instructors proudly claim to be Marxist, they cannot wean themselves from the middle class, i.e., bourgeois lifestyle that Marx noted must be destroyed in his revolution. The supreme irony is that in their classrooms and writings, many of these Marxist apparatchiks have earned a considerable amount of notoriety and wealth scorning the same evil Capitalist institutions that support them.

After those discoveries, I decided to enter the profession. I knew I could do better. I could implement into my classroom true diversity, the very principles that I witnessed were being blatantly disregarded. I could teach in a manner that demonstrated intellectual balance and honesty, trying not to show my own particular bias in the classroom. As noted below, the path was not an easy one, but for the sake of my own peace of mind and in fairness to my students, it had to be done.

So after twenty years of teaching at various colleges, here is my tale. Along the way, I would also utilize some of my students—not for indoctrination—but to provide balance and diversity to the classroom. Others who were not utilized in this manner still impacted my classroom—some negatively. Nevertheless, all are indelibly etched in my memory, and I bequeath their stories below.

But before we get to that end, we must first begin where my education germinated, at my grandmother's farm many years ago.

PART I
Abuelita's Farm: Cows, Chickens, and Culture

CHAPTER 1
Rise and Shine, Cabrones!

I grew up in Kerman, a rural community in Fresno County. Kerman is a small California town, primarily agricultural and situated in the center of the vast plain of the San Joaquin Valley. Like many towns in the valley, Kerman is also diverse in population: Americans of Mexican, Irish, German, Scandinavian, Italian or Russian descent, and other ethnicities are represented there; also growing in numbers recently in Kerman and throughout the valley is Indian Sikh.

My family's roots are Mexican-American; and most of our family lived in proximity of each other. When I was growing up, my parent's house was only a quarter of a mile from my maternal grandmother's farm. In the summer, our mother, in an attempt to establish a cultural bond and a work ethic with our grandmother or *Abuelita* as she was known to us, would rouse my brother Rick and me at the break of dawn to do work on her farm. But first, Mom had to get us out of bed.

Mom was the first to awaken in the morning, and we could usually hear her doing her work around the house. As she passed by our room, she would first give a couple of light taps on our closed door and quietly say, "OK, guys, time to get up."

That tepid attempt to rouse us out of bed was usually fruitless. Rick and I were then awake but all that accomplished was to make us turn over face down, grab our pillows over our heads, and hope in vain that the bad lady would go away. We were just kids wanting to enjoy the summer. While many of our friends were vacationing and spending a fun and leisurely summer break, we wondered why we had to get up to work at the break of dawn. What was the purpose of that enforced labor? We weren't getting paid. Additionally, Dad had a job, and we had a roof over our heads—wasn't that enough?

Well apparently, not for Mom because in a few minutes, she passed by our room again. And with her patience wearing thin, Mom knocked on the door louder and with a stentorian voice, barked into the closed door, "Hey, guys, *ya es tiempo*, get out of bed!"

Still Rick and I were dallying in our beds with intermittent yawns and stretching, but that was about it. We were still groggy and horizontal, and we wished to remain that way. What was needed to rouse us out of bed was "the encroachment," whereby Mom, thoroughly worked into a red-faced lather, burst into the room stamping mad like a bull. Lurching toward the window, Mom angrily drew the curtains completely open, flooding the room with the other unwanted intruder, the blinding morning sunlight. Then Mom punctuated the histrionics with her signature move—wheeling around like a battleship about to deliver a broadside. Mom then fired her salvo at us from pointblank range "*Levantarse cabrones*! What do you think I am running here, *un hotel de verano?*"

With Mom's payload delivered, we had no choice but to finally get out of bed. Reluctantly, we took off our pajamas and put on our work jeans, T-shirts, socks, and shoes—we didn't even bother to bathe; we knew what awaited us. Rick and I then walked out the door into the crisp morning air and began the quarter of a mile trek to Abuelita's house. Rubbing the sleep from our eyes, we walked east, guided by the breaking dawn—an illuminated path to our dreaded day of toil.

CHAPTER 2
The Udder Imbroglio of a Cow Hand

After our early morning arrival, Abuelita usually greeted us on her farm. Her appearance rarely varied unless she had a doctor's appointment; in which case, she dressed up nominally. Apart from the rare excursion from her farm, Abuelita rarely changed her garb because she, like us, needed to be properly dressed for the day's chores.

Typically, we would find our Abuelita in her usual attire: an old tattered and faded floral cotton print dress and apron usually stained with sweat, Crisco shortening, flour, and the remnants of whatever else she was conjuring up in her kitchen for the day's meals. Abuelita also wore a pair of black cat-eye glasses and crowned her head with a bandanna in which she tied her braided waist-length serpentine black and grey hair with hairpins. Tightly encasing her varicose-veined legs like a pair of sausages were her tan support hose rolled up to her knees. Her fifth appendage was a splintering brown wooden cane with which she supported her concaved frame and also used as a pointer to command her minions, Rick and I, the tasks to be done.

After entering Abuelita's kitchen, she would fortify us with a hearty meal for the day's work; the fare usually included refried beans, Spanish rice, potatoes, scrambled eggs, bacon, *chicarrones*, and stacks of steaming freshly-made flour tortillas wrapped in paper towels and bundled with a cotton cloth to keep them warm.

With our bellies filled, Rick and I would accompany our step-grandfather or *Tata*, as he was known to us, to begin the day's work. Tata also had his garb for the farm. His tall and lean frame was clothed in a sweat-stained T-shirt, khakis, boots, and a frayed straw hat that no longer blocked out the sun.

Tata would lead us to a small room attached to the garage where we prepared for the first task of the day, milking the cows. It was there that Tata invigorated himself with his own concoction for the day's work. In a ritual that never ceased to amaze me, Tata would take six raw eggs and break each one methodically, pouring the viscous contents into an empty milk bottle. With the intact yokes suspended in the jar like a lava lamp, Tata would raise the bottle to his lips, tilt his head back, open his mouth as if on a hinge, and unceremoniously drain the entire contents into his thirsty gullet. It was a spellbinding sight. I would stand in front of him transfixed—ironically with my mouth agape as well in sheer amazement—as Tata's mouth and throat worked like a well-lubricated machine, consuming the contents gluttonously. As Tata chugged, the thick mucus-like eggs leaked and dripped slowly down the sides of his mouth, but the machine continued, and Tata would wipe his mouth on his bare forearms only after the bottle was drained completely.

After that spectacle, we prepared the implements and trekked to the other side of the farm to milk the cows. The drill was known and followed by all, cows and humans alike. By the time we arrived at the milking house—a dilapidated structure of brick, concrete, and wood—the cows had already gathered at the gate, pushing each other, eager to be let in. The cows knew what awaited them—a tasty grain treat while we milked them. Rick and I would dispense a coffee can full of grain into each concrete trough space and wait for Tata to open the gate. And when the gate opened, it was every bovine and human for themselves; a ministampede ensued, and we made sure to say clear of the melee. Once the cows found the grain, we locked their necks into place with wooden braces, rendering them unable to escape so we could proceed with the milking.

Although confined in place, milking the cows by hand was a daunting and sometimes dangerous task, requiring speed, dexterity, and the ability to read a cow's mind through its actions. If we were not successful in prognosticating the intentions of a cow by its activity and then taking the immediate appropriate reaction, we paid the price. Obviously, the primary task was to milk the cows as quickly as possible without damage to ourselves or to the beast. But working on a cow's four teats with only two human hands placed us at a numerical disadvantage. Tata taught us to pull on the teats from the base to the tip until the pair became flaccid then move on to the other two, alternating until the cow was drained of milk. To the uninitiated, that might seem as an easy task; nevertheless, there were hazards to avoid that impeded the chore greatly.

For example, some cows were restless and soon tired of their entrapment quickly especially after their grain was gone. The impatient ones would jerk their heads back violently and try and pull themselves free from their locks followed by a seismic shaking of bodies and shifting of hind legs. The danger of those boisterous bovines manifested itself to me early in my rookie phase of milking; focusing on only those swollen teats and ignoring everything else with the blank single-mindedness of a tortoise on a lettuce hunt, I disregarded my cow's hoof dance until a bone-crushing pain pierced my foot as my toes compressed between hundreds of pounds of cow flesh and the concrete floor. Screaming in torment, I yanked my foot away and tore off my shoe and socks to see two formerly pink toenails splintered in half and turning purple rapidly. I limped in pain for almost a week—but I learned my lesson. I became trained to keep one eye on those roving hooves. Nevertheless, there were other lurking dangers to avoid as well.

Active tails were also a peril. Usually, tail activity increased in proportion to the amount of flies present. Sufficiently irritated, an agitated cow would work its tail back and forth methodically like a metronome on a piano. Keeping an eagle eye out for the movement was prudent because a swishing tail was a weapon. Again, due to my myopic milking, I once took a direct stab in the orb with a cow's tail; the needlelike hair produced a galaxy of exploding stars in my eye accompanied by a pulsating headache that tormented me for the balance of the day.

Nevertheless, the most dreaded regular event and certainly the most repugnant was the combination bovine bowel movement and urine shower. Inevitably during the milking, one or more cows would heed the call of nature and once again, experience was the key. After being on the receiving end of one of these events, I could then anticipate the explosion; the cow's hind quarters would tense with the back legs buckling toward the ground accompanied by a gravity-defying tail lift. That indicated that an eruption was imminent, and it was time to grab the milk bucket and rapidly seek cover. Some cows were like geysers, expelling their hot urine with tremendous force as it bounced off the concrete floor in all directions, showering everything in proximity. The defecation splatter was equally corrosive, particularly if the cow was diarrheic, which expanded the impact radius even more. A lava-like flow of hot fecal matter pours and splatters out of an ailing cow seemingly without abatement, triggering the inevitable reaction by my brother. Rick gagged and covered his mouth as he exerted all of his willpower to keep Abuelita's breakfast down.

Not to be outdone, the milk house imbroglio usually ended with Tata's *coupe de grâce*. With the cows drained of milk, fecal matter, and urine alike, my step-grandfather pulled out his member in full view of humans and animals and proceeded to pee, marking his property with a yellow shower of his own on the concrete floor. By doing that, he was showing the cows "See, I can do this too."

CHAPTER 3
What to Seize First, the Chicken or the Egg?

After the cows, the next task was collecting eggs from the chickens. Although the chickens were smaller creatures to handle, they still presented a formidable challenge. The chickens were kept in a large twenty by thirty-five foot pen, and within that was the smaller coop where the chickens laid their eggs.

Collecting chicken eggs could generate into chaos very quickly. The level of chicken agitation depended on the temperament of the birds and whether or not they were willing to surrender their eggs willingly. So I took a large basket and bravely enter the domain of the nesting fowl; standing in the doorway, I survey the scene and adjust my senses to the poultry world. The atmosphere was dark, and the air was thick with the amalgamated smell of damp, rotting wood, molting feathers, hay, and excrement.

Undaunted, I worked methodically under each nested hen in their hay-padded wooden box. Some chickens were impassive as I grabbed their eggs. Others deceptively conveyed the impression of passivity when suddenly, a lightning strike from their beak pierced my fingers, sometimes drawing blood in the process. A chicken *coup de main* was intrinsically painful, but if through my injury there was no egg to be found, my throe was augmented by anger.

As with other tasks on the farm, I learned through trial and error, which usually meant the quicker the better. I learned to work more deftly and seized the egg before the offended bird could strike. Despite my increased skill as I work my way through the nests, the environment within the chicken house intensified as more hens had their personal space invaded and potential offspring seized. Not unlike the defecating cows, one cackling hen triggered another. The more feathers flew, the more thick pungent air I inhaled.

Egg collection calamity was a given, but what was guaranteed to raise the din even higher was the order from Abuelita for fresh chicken on the dining table. The job required all hands. Rick and I were given the task of capturing the quarry, Tata prepared for the execution, and Abuelita readied for the cleaning of the hen and the meal.

Unfortunately, the order for the chicken collar usually came in the early afternoon when the hens were eating in the larger pen rather than nesting. Initially, Rick and I would chase the largest and tastiest-looking fowl—that usually proved fruitless. After our inevitable first miss at capture, all hell would break loose; the wing-flapping intensified, sending airborne more dust, feathers, and fecal matter. And in the large pen, the semi-free range hens had a decided advantage with ample room to dodge our attempts at ensnarement. Missing multiple targets, the dust cloud level in the pen would rise to an almost impenetrable haze. As exhaustion set in, it was time to switch to Plan B.

Hands on hips and hyperventilating, Rick and I staggered to a neutral corner of the pen to catch our breath and allow the chickens to settle. As the haze dissipated, we stalked our meal slowly, step by step like cheetahs in the Serengeti. In proximity of the fowl, we executed a desperate horizontal lunge and with grasping fingers, hoped to snag at least one stick-like leg.

Finally, we captured our prey. Holding our victim upside down by the legs, Rick and I emerged from the pen and proudly presented our prize to Tata, who usually just grunted in acknowledgement of our hard-fought victory. The hen craned its head upward, looking at us in bewilderment as we passed it from our hands to the executioner. Its puzzlement was answered immediately as Tata unceremoniously placed its head on a small wooden block and with one swing of a blood-stained hatchet, beheaded the bird quickly. If the implements were not handy, then Tata grabbed the chicken by the neck, gyrated it, and using his free hand, separated the bird with one sharp snap. The deed done, Tata dropped the body to the ground.

The headless hen rose to walk one final time, resurrected by the dying electrical charges haphazardly misfiring throughout the corpse accompanied by a fountain of blood pulsating into the air with every aimless step it took. Quickly the throbs of blood diminished in force and the chicken dropped, legs merely twitching as the electrical current abated. The blood flow trickled to a drop, and the quivering claws ceased movement—the last flutter of life from our once elusive catch.

Abuelita then picked up the bird and took it to the kitchen sink where she plucked, prepared, and cooked it, eventually ending up on our plates and into our bellies as fuel for more work on her farm.

****

Other chores ensued, e.g., setting irrigation pipes; feeding the hogs; tending goats; shoveling grain; picking grapes, cucumbers, strawberries, blackberries, figs, apples; and finally my most nauseating task, picking green worms from Abuelita's tomato plants. I would fill a small bucket with those vile creatures with their green slime and ghastly odor intensifying as the bucket filled. When the time came to empty the contents, I gagged as Rick did with the defecating cows. Those repugnant green tomato worms haunt me to this day: I still cannot eat fresh tomatoes picked from the vine.

CHAPTER 4

You Say, "Peenso," I Say, "Pencil," Let's Call the Whole Thing off

At the completion of those tasks, Rick and I retire to Abuelita's living room to deliver an account of the successes and failures of the day. The living room contained most of what Abuelita and Tata needed to spend the balance of their waking hours in repose—a television set, coffee, and cigarettes by the carton.

Setting foot into their living room was like entering the Los Angeles basin on a stagnant smoggy summer afternoon. Stratified layers of thick blue and black smoke hung heavy in the air, and anyone entering needed to brace themselves against the invasive and carcinogenic atmosphere. It was not unlike the chicken coop after a death chase except the air was clouded with tobacco smoke, not chicken matter. Generating the noxious fog were two human smoking machines well-fortified for the task. Each had at their side cigarette packs, lighters, and overflowing ash trays, the detritus of their ravenous addiction. Combined, Abuelita and Tata inhaled about two cartons of Tareyton 100's cigarettes per week, a Herculean task executed by geriatrics apparently fortified with iron lungs.

Through burning and watering eyes, Rick and I complete our litany of the day's work; after which, I sit and watch Mexican television for a while, accompanied by Abuelita's running commentary.

"*Cabrones Gabachos.*" Abuelita convulses, shaking her head at the latest news story. Spewing venom at the *gringos* was a frequent habit of hers as she literally smoked and fumed over the latest injustice imposed on her people by their white oppressors in North America. Abuelita was from Mexico, and although she had lived in the United States for many years, she never assimilated into North American life, (e.g., her knowledge of English was almost non-existent). Abuelita knew only two words in English, "potato chip," which she spoke in a pronounced accent.

Wanting to impress me with her mastery of the lexicon, Abuelita would occasionally sing to me, "Poo-taay-too-cheep," smiling and swinging a sliver of spud in front of my face. Only one time did she express to me a serious interest in learning English.

"*Ensename Ingles,*" Abuelita commanded to me one afternoon.

So I picked up a pencil from the countertop and showed it to her.

"Pencil," I said.

"*Pendejo?*" Abuelita gasped in wide-eyed shock.

"No, no, Abuelita, pencil," I articulated carefully.

"Peeen-so." She squinted at the pencil to focus then looked at me for affirmation.

"No, pencil."

"Peeenso."

"Pencil."

"Peeenso."

After a few minutes being trapped in that linguistic cul-de-sac, we wisely terminated the lesson and the topic is never broached again.

Tata was almost the same; the one English phrase he knew was "Whatsa matta you!" which he delivered with considerable force whenever Rick or I committed some egregious act on the farm. But at least Tata's English had a practical application. Other than that, he remained mostly silent even in Spanish.

After the day's television viewing, Tata shuffled to the foyer, stretched out horizontally in a reclining chair, and took a nap. Before pulling his straw hat over his eyes, Tata placed a transistor radio on his lap and cranks it to full volume.

Tata was immobile and apparently asleep, but how he managed to slumber was beyond comprehension because reverberating off the walls were crooners, trumpets, guitars, and other cacophonous reports of over-modulated Mariachi music. And there was no respite because between songs, hyperbolic Mexican pitchmen shrilled into the microphone, peddling everything from piñatas to Ford Pintos.

"Venga, venga, venga, a AutoMaxx!" echoed off the walls as the radio station segued into another chime silver-tongued by Vicente Fernandez.

After saying good-bye to Abuelita, Rick and I cringed from the din as we walked by Tata. We tapped on his dirty boots as we passed, but he was as immobile as the dead. We simultaneously raised our eyebrows in mock surprise at Tata's inertness, opened the door, and began the trek home.

"That was fun, huh?" Rick sighed sarcastically.

"Yeah, I can't wait for tomorrow," I concurred, shaking my head.

CHAPTER 5

From Commie to Cocoanut: My Betrayal to *La Raza*

Looking back on my formative years at Abuelita's farm, the intent of that experience becomes clear. When Mom burst into our bedroom to rouse us at the break of dawn, her primary motivation was not to instill into us a work ethic. Rather, by sending us to Abuelita's farm through those many summer years, Mom's intent was for us to spend time with Abuelita, and through that, Mom hoped Abuelita's culture and politics would be absorbed by us.

One of those means of conveyance was when sitting in that smoke-laden living room, Abuelita and I would obediently watch Univision or the local Spanish-speaking news channel, waiting with bated breath for the story that would hold us riveted to the screen. Immersed in the blazing hot summers of the San Joaquin Valley, we knew it was coming—it was only a matter of time. And when it was delivered, the story was usually broadcast in a familiar vein.

Appearing first was the news anchor, speaking forebodingly into the camera as if announcing the Apocalypse, a laboring farm worker suffered a heatstroke or other farm-related injury and had to be rushed to the hospital for immediate care. Next came a camera shot of the journalist *mise-en-scène*, and for prurient purposes, it was usually a young and hour-glass shaped Latina poured into a form-fitting blouse and displaying canyons of cleavage while breathlessly relating more details on the damnable injury. Cut away to a brief tear-inducing interview with the victim's family, it was followed by a panoramic camera shot of protesting activists, many holding up the familiar red, black, and white colors of the United Farm Workers Union (UFW), the esteemed and self-proclaimed non-violent turn-the-other-cheek defenders of the oppressed.

Then the story usually shifted to a local college and a somber interview with a humanities or social science professor, where the academic—grandiloquently framed by banks of tomes—lamented the incident with pontifical scorn and would target his wrath on the institution ultimately responsible for this crime, capitalism.

Finally, the solution was delivered by the academic that the United States should emulate more enlightened and humane societies (e.g., Fidel Castro's Cuba or some other Communist state) because they were the protectors of the downtrodden workers in order to make sure that "This does not happen again."

The interview ended with the journalist and academic nodding their heads in agreement, and I turned to see the inevitable. Abuelita was nodding as well, culminating with her raising and shaking with her withered fist into the air and yelling at the television, "*Viva Fidel!* Yaunkees *Bandidos!*"

It was a convincing spectacle. Farm workers, journalists, academics, and Abuelita were all politically united in a just cause. How could we possibly be wrong?

****

As my brother and I grew, our contact with Abuelita diminished. We were working in our Father's gasoline station and no longer had time to visit or labor with her frequently. Then I enrolled at Fresno State University. And although the predominant academic dogma of the university promoted the same pedagogy, my journey into the academic world would produce a political and cultural metamorphosis within me. Eventually, the world that had been presented to me through Abuelita's eyes and others would be tarnished by my own intellectual inquiry and growth.

When I had the chance, I returned to Abuelita's farm to eagerly tell her of my change. Her initial happiness upon seeing me turned to scorn quickly as I informed her of my newfound enlightenment. Naively, I thought that as eager as she was to teach me, Abuelita in turn would be receptive to my transforming views. Unfortunately, I soon found out Abuelita was not desirous to be reeducated; she had no toleration for any deviation from her views.

"*Cola prieta*," she would spew at me, Black Ass. In Abuelita's eyes, I had committed the cardinal sin—I was a betrayer to our race, our *raza*. Short of being a child rapist or a serial killer, there was nothing worse than that.

My mom reacted similarly. "*Mijo*, what has *happened* to you? What *books* are you *reading*?" she wailed and almost cried. For my mom and Abuelita, my transformation was antithetical to everything they had taught me. I had betrayed them politically and culturally in the worst possible way—I no longer thought as they did. And it did not end there. As my inquiry led in many different directions and I began to question the untouchable sacred cows of the Chicano movement, the racial epitaphs heaped on me intensified. From activists, students, and even educators alike the denunciations continued, "What are you, a Republican? How can you think like that, you are a Mexican, right?" As I stuck to my guns and tried to convince my detractors there were at least two sides to every story, the line of reasoning was usually met with the typical bromidic backlash, "You are nothing but a *cocoanut*!" For those not conversant, that translated to "Brown on the outside, White on the inside." Despite those salvos from family, friends, and educators alike, I continued on my quest for knowledge and diversity of thought. For me, it was the beginning of my new education as a student and as a teacher.

PART II

Fresno State University: From Indoctrination to Revelation

CHAPTER 6
Histrionics in Bob's Class: I Scream, You Scream, We All Scream for Ice Cream

Because of my experience at Abuelita's farm, the humanities and social sciences intrigued me, so I enrolled in a number of courses in Sociology and History. Not surprisingly, most of these courses echoed the familiar theme of capitalist and minority oppression.

Typical of those courses was a class led by Dr. Robert Fischer, who taught undergraduate Sociology. Bob, as he preferred to be addressed did not fit the stereotypical professorial mold. I saw him for the first time at the beginning of the semester, and when he entered the classroom, I assumed he was a returning older student, mainly because of his casual attire: T-shirt, cut-off and tattered blue jean shorts, flip-flop sandals, a shock of uncombed hair—a tangled mass of long and untrimmed Karl Marx-type beard, and a backpack sporting a large peace symbol. In short, Bob looked like he had just emerged from the activist 1960s.

Bob looked informal and also conducted his class in the same way. Instead of addressing the students from the lectern at the front of the class in the traditional manner, Bob placed the entire class in an egalitarian circle, and during the course of the semester, he would sit in different places in it—intimating that any particular spot that he would occupy consistently would give him an air of authority, a perception he attempted to avoid.

In that same vein of perceived egalitarianism, Bob actively engaged the class in sharing teaching assignments. Rarely did he lecture to the class. Despite that veneer of neutrality and diversity, Bob indoctrinated the class in a more surreptitious manner. Bob assigned all topics on which we were to research and present to our classmates and as the semester progressed, it became clear that those topics reflected Bob's politics of class and racial oppression in the United States of America. Through his assigned topics and brief lectures, it became apparent that according to Bob, the United States was the cause of all injustice, oppression, and poverty in the world. In the entire semester, there was not a single assigned topic pertaining to the Union of Soviet Socialist Republics (USSR) or Fidel Castro's Cuba or any other Communist state where these types of oppression might occur.

The semester proceeded without significant incident until the emotional apex of the student presentations was delivered by one of my fellow students. Her topic was the welfare state in America, and not surprisingly as she prepared for her spiel to the class, I already knew in which direction her presentation was headed.

I accurately made that assumption based on her appearance. Like instructor Bob, she was white, middle-aged, and she wore the classic hippie-chick garb from the Haight-Asbury district in San Francisco in the sixties—tie-dyed T-shirt, a long ground-sweeping coarse cotton skirt, and bespangled with a garish amount of Native American turquoise jewelry (e.g., earrings, necklaces, bracelets, and anklets) all of which made a cacophonous, migraine-inducing sound whenever she moved. Crowning her features was her hair, frizzed out and spiked in all directions—a gravity-defying mane reminiscent of Frankenstein's bride. She matched perfectly with Bob.

As her presentation began, the Hippie woman slowly but methodically worked herself into an agonizing emotional state. For many minutes with Bob inciting her on by nodding his head in constant approval like an electrified bobble-head doll, she blamed America for all her problems.

"I am a divorced mother of three," she commenced.

"My no-good-for-nothing drunken husband could not hold a job for more than a month," she scoffed.

"So because he could not remain sober and hold a job I left his sorry ass." She began to shake, and the Native American jewelry began to rattle.

"But I did not have a job and money, so I did the only thing I could in my situation, I applied for freakin' welfare," she spewed.

"Have any of you young pups ever apply for welfare?" That inquiry was followed by a monumental pregnant pause as her head swiveled around the classroom circle, eyes wide open and seeking affirmation. When none came, she shouted to the ceiling, "Don't!"

"Let me tell you why the welfare system is so demeaning," she continued.

"You go there, and they make you sit around and wait and wait and wait. Then they make you fill out a bunch of forms, asking everything from your income to your last bowel movement." She cackled a mirthless laugh. But not a sound was heard in response as everyone by then was immobilized by the spectacle.

"And after all that humiliation, what do you get? A handful of change. These freakin' capitalists are all the same. They make you beg and beg for a pittance. Don't be fooled! We live in an oppressive society. I barely had enough money for the essentials. After all my humiliation, it is this system, this society, in which at the end of the month, a single mother of three did not have enough money for one single ice cream cone for my kids!"

By that time, the hippie woman was shouting and crying in spasms, and her emotional-laden jerks intensified the noise of her tinseled body. Then she dropped her head on her desk, covered her arms over her head, and sobbed uncontrollably.

Rising from his egalitarian position in the classroom circle, Bob slowly and dramatically walked from his seat to the vanquished woman and in a grand gesture of solidarity, placed his hand on her shoulder like the pontiff giving a benediction. And with her presentation ended and the climax reached, Instructor Bob magnanimously dismissed the class for the day.

I then exited the classroom and walked toward the Student Union, plagued by questions. I began immediately to reflect upon the emotional outburst that I just witnessed, and also to question the significance of the entire event. The hippie woman's outburst was certainly forceful. But were her histrionics justified? I understood her situation was not easy, and I was sure money was tight. And of course, any trip to the welfare office must entail some degree of humiliation for most people. And finally, it must have been demeaning not being able to buy ice cream for her children at the end of the month. But really, *so what?* The bottom line was her kids did not starve. Surely, many people had gone through similar deprivations, but they survived. Was it really a poignant example of oppression and injustice in America? And what was dogging me the most was why did Instructor Bob so blatantly endorse the Hippie woman's lament about oppressive capitalism and her inability to afford ice cream for her children?

I began to mull over Bob's course in its entirety and questioned what he emphasized in class for the remainder of the semester. Nevertheless, I was still willing to give those like-minded instructors the benefit of the doubt. So next, I enrolled in Dr. Elizabeth Hartung's class on Social Inequality.

CHAPTER 7
Social and Racial Inequality in Beth's Class: Scrub that Tub, Mammy, and Don't Forget to Call me Ma'am

As I soon learned, Beth, as she preferred to be called, like Bob expressed a similar political ideology, and her course reflected many of the topics assigned in Bob's class.

A prime example was a book we were obligated to read, analyze, and ultimately spend a considerable amount of class time on, *Between Women: Domestics and Their Employers* by Judith Rollins. Ms. Rollins interviewed twenty employers, twenty domestics, and she herself participated in domestic work for the evidence in her book.

The core of her argument is that capitalist systems have "institutional inequality" which includes "interpersonal rituals" that reinforce acceptance of inequality. Consequently, the nucleus of her book is to look at these forms of oppression that manifest themselves into the relationship between black female domestic servants and their white female employers[2]

Rollins begins with a detailed look at the history of domestic service, particularly during the Industrial Revolution and the emerging capitalist West, and then focuses on modern America: "The distinct pattern of domestic service in twentieth-century America... appears to be directly related to racism, not only through the exclusion of these women from other jobs, but also by the prevention of men of color from obtaining wages sufficient to support their families.[3]

Since these women are stuck in their jobs and there is no escape, they have to cope under these conditions of subservience. Rollins then proceeds with her litany of oppression. The older domestics Rollins interviewed chronicled the physical ailments associated with their labor: lower back problems, varicose veins, and ankle and foot injuries.[4] These physical ailments are accompanied by the forms of deference and subservience that Rollins asserts is "the essence of the employer-domestic relationship".[5] These forms of deference include the white female employer calling their domestics by their first name, and by contrast, the domestic employee is obligated to call their employers by their last name. Employers also refer to their domestics as "girls" regardless of age, and employers prefer to be called, "Ma'am."[6] Another form of deference is that "the domestic does not initiate touching her employer and is careful to respect the private space around the employer's body by maintaining distance."[7]

Finally, the fact that the domestic is black and the employer is white strengthens the employers' ego by enforcing racial stereotypes. The white employer, by having a black domestic, is displaying to the world that she can afford paid help at home merely by the fact that the domestic is black—a white domestic might be mistaken for an acquaintance and therefore neutralize her demonstration of affluence and racial separation to the world.[8] According to Rollins, the forms of deference that typified the domestic-employer relationship is a microcosm of a larger, "world-wide stratification pattern" that is typical of black-white relationships throughout the capitalist world.

As noted above, in Beth's class, we spent a considerable amount of time on this work, examining in excruciating detail the forms of oppression as outlined by Rollins. As the class sessions dragged on, I had a flashback to Bob's class and the ice cream tale: *why are we spending so much time on these trivialities?* Is it *really* a form of oppression if an employer calls her worker by her first name? Is it *really* a form of oppression if the domestic has to respect an employer's personal space? Is it *really* a form of oppression if a domestic is black and their work in a white household is *seen* by the outside world as a status symbol? *In a class entitled Social Inequality, is this the best example of inequality that can be presented?*

These questions and more hounded me internally as Beth's class dragged on, but I said nothing. Then while immersed in our meticulous dissection of Rollins's work, Steve, a classmate, interrupted Beth in mid-lecture.

"Are these stories really a form of oppression?" Steve asked Beth.

Stunned silence permeated the classroom as Steve voiced what I was sure many, not only I, was thinking.

Sensing that he hit pay dirt, Steve pressed his argument further as he looked around the room for affirmation and let Rollins's book drop on his desk as an object of little worth.

"I mean, aren't there other more oppressive systems in the world besides the United States? Isn't there a lot of oppression in Communist countries like the Soviet Union?"

Beth then jumped in.

"Yes, there have been some problems with human rights in Communist countries, but mostly, these were only mistakes. Whenever capitalism or a monarchy is disposed and a new system that is sympathetic to the worker is put in place, some adjustments have to be made, OK? So let's get back to Rollins's work now."

With that, Steve's sagacious remark was dismissed, and we proceeded as Beth instructed. Beth's justification was that *mistakes* and *adjustments* had to be made in order to usher in a more worker-friendly system.

****

Chastised, Steve remained silent throughout the remainder of the semester, but my interest was piqued. So one week later, I ventured into the Henry Madden Library at Fresno State and approached a librarian.

"Where are your books on Communism—specifically Soviet Communism?"

The librarian escorted me to a section holding those stacks.

"Are you looking for a specific author?" she asked

"No, but I am looking mainly for writings from the victims of Communism," I replied.

"Well, this section right here might help you," she said and left.

I scanned the stacks of books until I saw it, *The Gulag Archipelago* by Alexander Solzhenitsyn. Because I was a student of history, I had heard the name and knew he had spent years in the Soviet gulag, but I had not read his work and none of my professors had mentioned it in class—much less used it. So I had dismissed it as a work of no consequence. As I pulled out volume 1, I noted a fine layer of dust had encased the book. Solzhenitsyn's work was literally gathering physical and intellectual dust on the stacks.

I hesitated—but I continued. I had to know. I took the book, went to a desk, and began to read, and what I would discover in those pages would be beyond my worst conceivable nightmare.

CHAPTER 8

Soviet Communism: Working Men of all Countries Unite, You Have Nothing to Lose but Your Lives! Discovery and Revelation

As I read *The Gulag Archipelago* and other works on the USSR, the immensity and scope of the crimes within the Soviet Union became apparent to me in all its gruesome detail.

Solzhenitsyn chronicled a nation so despotic that its fiendish tentacles stretched and impacted negatively almost every Soviet citizen with its brand of oppression. Following the Bolshevik Revolution in December 1917, Vladimir Lenin, one of the founders of the Soviet State, was contemplating the confiscation of property, imprisonment, and forced labor for all who opposed Bolshevik law—only one month after the Communist takeover in Russia.[9] To execute that doctrine in January 1918, Lenin called on all agencies of the Soviet Union to "purge the Russian land of all kinds of harmful insects."[10] Consequently, that unconscionable policy was carried out faithfully by Lenin's enforcement organizations, mainly by the USSR's internal police, the *Cheka*, the predecessor to the Committee for State Security (KGB).

In September 1918, an army newspaper declared boldly, "Without mercy, without sparing, we will kill our enemies in scores of hundreds, let them be thousands, let them drown themselves in their own blood... let there be floods of blood of the bourgeois."[11] One official of the *Cheka*, Martin Ivanovich Latsis, described his task as thus: "We are not carrying out war against individuals. We are exterminating the bourgeoisie as a class. We are not looking for evidence or witnesses to reveal deeds or words against Soviet power. The first question we ask is—to what class does he belong, what are his origins, upbringing, education or profession? These questions define the fate of the accused."[12]

By late 1917, the *Cheka* was operating its first labor camps.[13] And from September to October 1918, the *Cheka* executed ten to fifteen thousand people. Consequently, within the timeframe of approximately eight weeks, "the *Cheka* alone had executed two to three times the total number of people condemned to death by the tsarist regime over ninety-two years."[14] Soviet agents were clandestine and ubiquitous. They portrayed themselves as doctors, meter men, railroad conductors, taxi drivers, bank tellers—virtually anyone in the public realm could be an agent.[15] Through that conversion method, Soviet agents seized and incarcerated citizens indiscriminately to fill labor quotas and simultaneously to intimidate and suppress the population.

Arrests led to interrogation, which were particularly heinous: "prisoners would have their skulls squeezed within iron rings; [they] would be lowered into an acid bath; they would be trussed up naked to be bitten by ants and bedbugs; a ramrod [would be] heated over a... stove [and]... thrust up their anal canal; a man's genitals would be slowly crushed beneath the toe of a jackboot; and in the luckiest of possible circumstances, prisoners would be tortured by being kept from sleeping for a week, by thirst, and by being beaten to a bloody pulp...."[16] Some *Chekas* specialized in certain types of torture. The

Kharkov *Cheka* indulged in scalping; the Voronezh *Cheka* placed their victims naked into a nail-studded barrel and rolled them around in it. The *Cheka* in Odessa chained military officers to wooden planks and then pushed them slowly into furnaces, burning them alive, or they immersed their victims first into a tank of boiling water then into freezing water then back into boiling water, repeating the process until the victim expired.[17]

Occasionally, prisoners sentenced to death were often placed in overcrowded cells to await their fate:

> In a cell intended for solitary confinement they would shove seven... sometimes ten, fifteen, even *twenty-eight* prisoners.... And they remained packed in this way for weeks or even *months*! People in these circumstances don't think about execution, and it's not being shot they worry about, but how to move their legs, how to turn over, how to get a gulp of air... and all of them *stood for several days so jammed in against each other* in one big cell that it was impossible either to raise or lower an arm.... [italics in the original].[18]

Feeding this mechanism of perdition was a system of law that interpreted crimes against the Soviet state so broadly that minor or inconsequential acts resulted in long stints of incarceration or death. In Article 58 and Article 6 of the Criminal Code of 1926, the Soviets decreed that any action or absence of action directed toward the weakening of state power was a counterrevolutionary offense. Consequently, the refusal of a prisoner in the gulag to work when in a state of starvation was a "weakening of state power" and punishable by execution.[19] Peasants were arrested for "taking a stalk of grain, a cucumber,... potatoes, a chip of wood, a spool of thread... all of whom got ten years"[in a labor camp].[20] In 1928 alone, approximately 1,400 "terrorist acts" by peasants, i.e., resistance to seizure of food, were reported by Soviet authorities.[21] A decade in prison was the punishment for the theft of potatoes, and the same sentence was given to a woman for picking ten onions from a collective farm. Death sentences were imposed for the theft of a couple of sheaves of corn.[22]

In one particularly tragic episode, another peasant with six children met a similar fate:

> Because he had six mouths to feed he devoted himself wholeheartedly to collective farm work, and kept hoping he would get some return for his labor. And he did—they awarded him a decoration. They awarded it at a special assembly, made speeches. In his reply, the peasant got carried away. He said, 'Now, if I could just have a sack of flour instead of this decoration! Couldn't I somehow?' A wolflike laugh rocketed through the hall, and the newly decorated hero went off to [the gulag], together with all six of those dependent mouths.[23]

CHAPTER 9

Soviet Communism: Working Men of All Countries Unite, You Have Nothing to Lose but Your Lives! The Gulag

The Soviet gulag was usually the end for those sent there. Some survived. Many did not. The "supreme law of the Archipelago" was articulated by Naftaly Frenkel, one of the early organizers of the gulag: "We have to squeeze everything out of a prisoner in the first three months—after that we don't need him anymore".[24]

Prisoners of the Soviet labor camps were forced to build various public works projects to produce the worker's paradise. Solzhenitsyn notes that the construction of the one hundred and forty mile Belomor Canal through rocky soil, boulders, and swamps was particularly oppressive. Under Stalin's orders, the canal had to be built within two years, from September 1931 to April 1933, and completed "cheaply".[25]

"Cheaply" meant tormenting and rudimentary labor. Boulders were excavated with a net or by wooden cranes. If neither saws nor axes were available, trees were leveled in a most primitive fashion: "Ropes were tied around the trees and they were rocked back and forth by brigades pulling in different directions—*they rocked the trees out*" [italics in the original].²⁶

Not surprisingly, those and other similar types of labor depleted the workforce quickly. Nevertheless, the incapacitated were not exempt from their duties. Those unable to walk to work by themselves were dragged on sledges by other laborers, or were hit with clubs and mangled by guard dogs. ²⁷ The Soviets ordered mass shootings for any slowdown in work. To spread terror rapidly, some camp commandants shot prisoners randomly.²⁸ Prisoners were also beheaded with axes or stabbed to death with picks and shovels.²⁹ In a sober testament to the grim reality of the labor camps, a Romanian prisoner, Michael Solomon, was brought before a camp doctor. The physician told Solomon, "Before being a doctor, I am a *Chekist*, and as such I must tell you that you are not brought here to live but to suffer and die.... If you live longer, it means that you are guilty of one of two things: either you worked less than was assigned or you ate more than your proper due."³⁰

Some who died on the worksite became a permanent fixture of the fruits of their labor. D. P. Vitkovsky, an eyewitness on the construction of the White Sea Canal, noted that some corpses left at their worksite were thrown into a concrete mixer and thus became a part of a canal lock at the city of Belomorsk.³¹

Death in the Soviet labor camps was also accelerated by other factors. In the summer, the workday was often lengthened to fourteen hours. Women wielded wheelbarrows filled with stones frequently in sixty-two hours of continuous work. ³² In the winter, labor proceeded despite temperatures between 50 to 60 degrees below zero Fahrenheit: work was cancelled only when the temperature was lower than 65 degrees below zero.³³

As noted above, prisoners were often executed systematically. At Adak, a camp on the Pechora River, the condemned had their mouths gagged and arms tied behind their backs. Then they were placed in carts and transported to the camp cemetery, where they were dumped into gigantic pits and buried alive.[34] An equally appalling practice involved the sinking of barges loaded with prisoners in the Gulf of Finland and in the White, Caspian, and Black Seas.[35] And beginning in June 1920 at the Kholmogory labor camp on the Drina River, prisoners "were often loaded onto barges, stones were tied around their necks, their arms and legs were tied, and they were thrown overboard into the river." [36]

Nevertheless, perhaps the most repugnant and tortuous weapon used by the Soviets against their own people was hunger. In the Kolyma labor camp, a remote region in eastern Siberia, "the prisoners were so famished that...they ate the corpse of a horse which had been lying dead for more than a week and which not only stank but was covered with flies and maggots."[37] Fiendishly, the Soviets expanded a policy of state-induced famine in other areas of the USSR to eradicate class divisions, resulting in a deliberate policy to exterminate millions of their own citizens.

CHAPTER 10
Soviet Union: Collectivization, Starvation, and Its Marxist Brood

Thirty years before he seized power in Russia, Lenin realized the power famine could wield in transforming Russian society: "Famine would... destroy faith not only in the tsar, but in God too."[38] To trigger the famine, a vast transformation in Russian society must first take place. In accordance with Marxist dogma in 1917, Lenin insisted that "private ownership of...land must be abolished"[39] Consequently, Russian peasants were placed in vast collective farms where production quotas were set by the Communists; additionally, a decree issued in May 1918 entitled "On the Monopoly of Food," empowered the Soviets to seize from the peasants any grain held in excess of those quotas. That resulted in the forcible collection of grain, and a state policy of deliberately allowing the peasant to starve was implemented. So in 1921, the first great famine killed five million Russians.[40]

Following his mentor, Dictator Joseph Stalin realized the power of those collectives. In 1933, Stalin said, "From the standpoint of Leninism, collective farms... taken as a form of organization, are a weapon, and nothing but a weapon."[41] So Stalin took that blueprint for genocide on an even grander scale. From 1929–1933, the Soviets expanded that policy to include the liquidation of a particular class of Soviet citizen, the kulak. The kulak was the theoretical Russian equivalent of the middle-class bourgeoisie (e.g., the moneylender, or individuals who were wealthier than the typical peasant). They found themselves in Stalin's crosshairs when in 1929, he exclaimed, "We must smash the kulaks, eliminate them as a class.... We must strike at the kulaks so hard as to prevent them from rising to their feet again.... Liquidate the kulaks as a class!"[42] So the Soviets started a policy of "dekulakization" (i.e., class genocide on these individuals along with the expansion of collective farms). The apex of this policy culminated in 1932–1933 when a quarantine and seizure of grain on the collectivized in the Ukraine was enforced due to peasant resistance and the perceived "hoarding" of food.[43]

At this point, it is important to note that the attempt by the Soviet Union to distinguish the kulaks as a class distinctive from the peasant was a nebulous one. As noted above, the kulaks were seen theoretically as *capitalists*, but their real distinction from the peasant class was almost non-existent. For example, in 1927, the most prosperous kulaks had approximately three cows and up to ten hectares upon which to farm for an average family of seven individuals.[44] That was hardly an economic bounty accumulated at the expense of exploiting the peasant masses. Moreover, in what can only be described as supremely ironic, "the average kulak's income was lower than that of the average rural official who was persecuting him as a representative of a wealthy class." [45]

In reality, those trifling class distinctions were of no real concern to the Soviets; they had a much broader plan in scope. In March 1933, due to the quarantine, citizens of Ukraine were famished: "When the snow melted true starvation began.... And now they ate anything at all. They caught mice, rats, sparrows, ants, earthworms. They ground up bones into flour, and did the same with leather and shoe soles; they cut up old skins and furs to make noodles of a kind, and they began to dig up the roots and eat the leaves and buds."[46] Starving peasants ate horse manure because it often contained grains of wheat.[47] In fact, Soviet officials became suspicious if peasants were *not* in a state of starvation: then the Soviets would conduct a thorough search, assuming that food had been hidden. One party member, convinced that a peasant was hoarding food, found a small bag of flour mixed with ground tree bark and leaves. The Soviet official then poured the contents into a nearby pond.[48]

And the horror continued. An eyewitness noted, "I saw people dying from hunger. I saw women and children with distended bellies, turning blue, still breathing but with vacant, lifeless eyes."[49] Others made the astute connection between the victims and those of the Nazis: "And the peasant children! Have you ever seen the newspaper photographs of the children in the German camps? They were just like that: their heads like heavy balls on thin little necks, like storks, and one could see each bone of their arms and legs protruding from beneath the skin… and the entire skeleton was stretched over with skin that was like yellow gauze."[50] Desperation induced parents into psychotic behavior; some mothers abandoned their children at someone's door on the delusional hope that someone would help.[51] Others succumbed to the abominable; there were parents that killed, cut up, cooked, and ate their own children.[52]

****

The facts demonstrate that the USSR embarked on a policy of Marxist social engineering almost unparalleled in human history. By the end of 1934, nine-tenths of the acreage sown in the Soviet Union was concentrated in approximately 240,000 collective farms which had replaced approximately twenty million family farms existing in 1929.[53] Under Stalin's reign, the entire operation of collectivization impacted approximately 105 million people.[54] Although the grain confiscation in Ukraine was halted in 1933, almost an entire generation of rural peasants and their children in the USSR—but especially in Ukraine—was destroyed or damaged permanently.

Mercilessly, while millions were dying of starvation, the Soviet Union actually *exported* grain, "Shipping 18 million hundredweight of grain abroad."[55] Consequently, from 1930–1937, the total number of peasants killed as a result of dekulakization and the Soviet-induced famine was approximately 14.5 million.[56]

And the carnage continued. As I sifted through the evidence, it became clear to me that the scope and scale of the decimation inflicted by the Soviet Union upon its own people was beyond anything I had imagined. Investigating further, Soviet suppression and terror permeated to its client state and neighbor, the Chinese Communists, who had their own revolution in 1949.

****

In August of 1919, Moscow initiated a successful plan of action and subversion in China lasting for thirty years, consisting of money, men, arms, and intelligence, which was also aided by the Second Sino-Japanese War; it culminated in bringing the Communists under Mao Tse-tung to power. Moscow began secretly training a Chinese army on Soviet soil while simultaneously establishing a vast network of espionage spearheaded by the GRU—the military intelligence for the USSR outside its borders—in major Chinese cities including Shanghai, Canton, and Beijing. Moscow also sent top-level Russian advisors to guide the Chinese Communist's military operations and training.[57]

The result was a stunning victory for international Communism. On October 1, 1949, Mao appeared standing on top of the iconic Tiananmen Gate in front of the Forbidden City and inaugurated the People's Republic of China (PRC). On that fateful day, Mao had established himself as the absolute ruler of approximately 550 million people.[58]

In Mao, the Russian Communists found an ideological disciple willing to emulate Stalin. Soviet leader Nikita Khrushchev observed, "When I look at Mao I see Stalin, a perfect copy."[59] Mao in turn kowtowed to the Soviet dictator as he gushed about Stalin: "Is Stalin the leader of the world revolution? Of course he is. Who is our leader? It is Stalin. Is there a second person? No. Every member of our Chinese Communist Party is Stalin's pupil… Stalin is the teacher to us all."[60] And as a pupil to Comrade Stalin, the record indicates he was a quick study. A concise overview of PRC ideology and terror reveal a pattern eerily similar to that of the Soviets.

Firstly, torture was gruesomely applied to anyone who resisted. In the Henan Province in 1949, those categorized as landlords were "shot, hanged, beheaded, battered to death, nailed to the walls of buildings or buried alive."[61] In Manchuria, Chinese men were tortured by having their testicles squeezed and crushed in bamboo pliers.[62] The tearing out of fingernails was also a common practice.[63] Other cases included women having their teeth pulled out before being hacked to death. Some victims had nails driven into their skulls; others had their tongues cut off and eyes gouged out.[64] Punishments for peasants caught "stealing" their own harvest included children having their fingers cut off, or having wires run through their ears and hung up by the wire from a wall.[65]

Secondly, with advice from Soviet gulag experts on management, Chinese labor camps were erected on the Russian model: a typical day in the camps consisted of a minimum twelve hours of work; four hours of political indoctrination, self-criticism, and mutual denunciation; one hour for meals; and a mere five hours of sleep. Prisoners often slept on the bare floor and were allowed one shower per month.[66] Many of those camps were located in the far north of China where winters were comparably as oppressive as in Siberia. The official term for the camps was *laogai*, or "reform through labor," and labor they did—in excess.[67] Communist leaders ordered the building of vast irrigation systems—dams, reservoirs, canals—utilizing the labor of 100 million peasants, who moved a quantity of earth and masonry equivalent to 950 Suez Canals, using mostly labor-intensive tools such as picks and shovels.[68] In sub-zero temperatures, prisoners dug the canals twelve to sixteen hours a day; a pair would typically carry loads of 330–430 lbs. of soggy earth on shoulder poles, up and down steep banks, literally hundreds of times daily.[69] Intellectuals who objected to Communist rule, including professors, headmasters and schoolteachers were also shipped to work in the camps.[70] Women were not spared either. In the province of Ningsia, 100,000 women dug 50,000 ditches in 1952 alone. Occasionally laboring at night, they competed these tasks often with children strapped to their backs.[71]

All laborers were given work quotas, but when the quotas were not met, food rations were reduced. With less food it was more difficult to continue working. Deranged with hunger, prisoners hunted living creatures for sustenance: mice, rats, snakes, lizards, worms, and even cockroaches were consumed; some even searched through the excrement of other prisoners for undigested grains to eat.[72]

Despite the decimation it caused to prisoners, the "Great Leap Forward" plan by Mao, launched in 1958 to rapidly industrialize China on Stalin's model was a disaster. Many projects had to be abandoned that were only halfway completed. For example, out of the over 500 large reservoirs initiated, 200 were discontinued after only one year of work.[73]

Thirdly, like the Ukrainian famine of the early 1930s, collectivization and starvation continued on Chinese soil. As a precursor to the other element of the "Great Leap Forward," in October 1955, Mao ordered the grouping of peasant co-operatives in numbers of up to 300 families, ultimately resulting in 400 million Chinese peasants forced into joining over 752,000 collectives.[74] With the state forcibly taking most of the food produced by the peasants in those collectives, starvation commenced. In 1955, Mao read reports of people resorting to eating tree bark, but he did little to relieve their suffering. And not surprisingly, the suffering intensified; after only one year, grain yields fell by at least 40 percent.[75]

The Chinese famine peaked from 1958–1961 where once again as what happened in Ukraine, cannibalism ensued, including incidents of parents eating their children. And as it occurred in the USSR, the Chinese Communists hoarded and exported grain as well. The famine suited Mao well. He callously remarked, "Deaths have benefits… they can fertilize the ground."[76] Some party officials took the statement literally when they ordered buried corpses to be exhumed, bodies removed, and the remains grounded up to be used as fertilizer.[77] So the dead were victimized again along with a prophetic warning from Mao for the living. In a statement made in Moscow, Mao ominously noted: "We are prepared to sacrifice 300 million Chinese for the victory of the world revolution."[78]

Mao fell short of his sacrificial goal during the four-year "Great-Leap Forward" experiment, only 38 million died.[79]

Despite a Sino-Soviet ideological split in 1960, the Marxist-Leninist-Stalinist strain of malignancy had been successfully passed into the Chinese body politic with all its attendant carnage attached. But the malignancy was not to end there; another disciple would emerge from this Marxist experiment.

****

In 1968, Mao began to ship arms to a little-known rebel group in Cambodia, the Khmer Rouge. Buttressed by its Communist neighbor to the North in 1975, the Khmer Rouge came to power in Cambodia and then proceed on an accelerated social engineering experiment that in its intensity exceeded even that of the Chinese. Immediately after his ascension to power, Mao congratulated its leader Pol Pot on his audacity: "You have scored a splendid victory. Just a single blow and no more classes."[80]

The *single blow* for the Khmer Rouge came in the wake of the United States' defeat and withdrawal of their combat troops in Southeast Asia. That opened the door for the Khmer Rouge led by a coterie of middle-class intellectuals calling themselves the *Angka Loeu* or "the Higher Organization." Their goal for the people of Cambodia was a complete transformation of society and individual alike. The plan included a "total social revolution" where the past was destroyed and to "psychologically reconstruct" individuals through "terror and other means," and then "rebuilding [the individual] according to party doctrines by substituting a series of new values."[81]

This transformation impacted the capital of Phnom Penh when on April 17, 1975, the Khmer Rouge ordered the entire city evacuated. All hospitals were forcibly vacated at gunpoint, displacing the sick and dying into the streets. Some patients even pushed others who were bedridden. All city records were destroyed, and all books were incinerated or thrown into the Mekong River. Possessions were confiscated, and those who lingered in Phnom Penh were executed.[82] In some sectors of Phnom Penh, individuals were given only ten minutes to vacate their property. During the exodus from the capital, the Khmer Rouge executed officers of the defeated Lon Nol government, along with other high-ranking officials. The death toll from the evacuation of Phnom Penh was approximately twenty thousand victims.[83]

Less than one week later, the Khmer Rouge began to evacuate other cities. In Siem Reap, over one hundred hospital patients were murdered in their beds with clubs and knives. Other groups targeted for execution were beggars, prostitutes, civil servants, and teachers. Often, entire families of the "guilty" were massacred to prevent "revenge."[84]

Within two months, four million people were forcibly relocated into the jungles to construct a new society, working fourteen to eighteen hours a day. That society consisted of cooperatives which grouped together several hundred people or a village, a smaller version of the Chinese communes.[85] In many communes, each person retained only one plate and one spoon.[86] As work intensified, sustenance became scarce. At one point in Southwestern Cambodia, one peasant noted that food for twenty peasants consisted only of one handful of rice boiled in a pot.[87] Those who could not work were not fed. As famine and disease spread, the old, infirm, and orphans were the first to die. That famine was exacerbated by the Khmer Rouge's practice of seizing and exporting tons of rice in exchange for arms.[88]

Executions were public, and relatives were forced to watch family members be garroted, decapitated, stabbed, or axed to death.[89] In some villages, children of about eight were taken from their families to work in children's labor brigades. Parents were notified when their children died; however, if the parents wept or showed distress at the news, they were brutally punished for displaying bourgeois sentimentality. The reasoning was their children had died for the revolution: they should be proud and not grieve.[90]

Anyone who broke a farm implement was accused of negligence and shot.[91] Occasionally, Khmer Rouge soldiers ate the livers of their victims; others slashed the throats of babies and children.[92] Pre-teenage students were forced to execute their teachers; former officials were mutilated then crucified.[93] Women had their breasts slashed, or hot irons were inserted into their vaginas.[94] Intellectuals not shot were forced to labor in the fields in shifts of at least twelve hours.[95] Any complaint warranted an execution. Khmer Rouge officials admitted to executing without due cause as one stated: "Better to kill an innocent person than to leave an enemy alive."[96]

When not working or witnessing executions, the Cambodians were subjected to "criticism and self-criticism" sessions led by Khmer

Rouge cadres, where peasants were singled out and berated for their "errors" while at work, similar to the Chinese sessions and the Soviet "show trials" under Stalin.[97]

Consequently, in less than two years, approximately 100,000 Cambodians were executed, 20,000 died trying to flee, 400,000 died in the forced removal from their homes, and a further 680,000 died in the rural villages: thus at least 1.2 million Cambodians lost their lives at the hands of the Marxists, fully 20 percent of the entire population.[98]

Leader Pol Pot was ecstatic. In an address to his people on September 27, 1977, he proclaimed: "For more than two thousand years our people lived in utter deprivation, in complete despair and hopelessness. What was the brightest day for them? It was 17 April 1975."[99]

****

Then there is my Abuelita's favorite, Fidel Castro and his reign in Cuba, which continues to this very day under the direction of his brother Raul. Although Fidel, who considered law as a possible vocation, attended Jesuit school in Havana and was a gifted athlete, the evidence indicated that Fidel was first and foremost a revolutionary.

A voracious reader, Fidel absorbed the works of Marx, Lenin, Adolf Hitler, Benito Mussolini, and Juan Peron. He quickly put their ideology into action when at the age of thirteen, he attempted to organize sugar workers against his own father;[100] and in 1947 participated in an abortive raid to overthrow Rafael Trujillo in the Dominican Republic. Brother Raul described Fidel as having a "very explosive nature";[101] and a contemporary of Fidel described him as a "power-hungry person, completely unprincipled, who would throw in his lot with any group he felt could help his political career."[102] Additionally, Fidel's anti-US sentiments appeared early in his political career at the Pan-American Conference in Bogota, Colombia. In 1948, Fidel protested against the US by dropping leaflets from a balcony condemning Yankee colonialism.

Also venomous toward Cuban leader Fulgencio Batista, on July 26 1953, Fidel and 160 revolutionaries attacked four military barracks in Moncada, Cuba, to ignite an armed uprising against Batista's troops. Outnumbered ten to one, the attack failed miserably, and Fidel was jailed.[103]

Batista, alarmed by this brazen assault, placed the army on full alert and embarked on a series of violent repressions. Fidel was given a swift trial and sentenced to fifteen years in prison. Ironically, Batista's repressive measures evoked sympathy for Fidel, and Fidel's public image as a romantic figure on the national and international stage grew.

Nevertheless, in a gesture of goodwill that he would soon regret, Batista declared amnesty for all political prisoners in May 1955. In a matter of weeks after his release, Fidel fled to Mexico to form and train a group of rebels to overthrow the Cuban leader.

In Mexico, Fidel formed an intimate friendship with Argentinian physician Ernesto "Che" Guevara. In Guevara, Fidel found a likeminded ideologue also versed in the works of Marx and Lenin who despised the profit-motive and believed in the perfectibility of man. Che noted that "revolution cleanses men, improving them as the experimental farmer corrects the defects of his plants."[104] Employing his version of Social Darwinism, Guevara said, "Revolutionary institutions... permit the natural selection of those who are destined to march in the vanguard, and who dispense rewards and punishments to those who fulfill their duty or act against the society under construction."[105] So in order to cleanse society of those who did not do their duty, Che believed that "a revolutionary must become a cold killing machine motivated by pure hate."[106]

Emboldened with Marxist fervor after months of training in Mexico, Fidel and his rebels, the *Fidelistas,* landed in Cuba on December 2, 1956. Sporadic skirmishes with Batista's forces compelled Fidel and his men to flee into the Sierra Maestra Mountains in Southern Cuba. Soon thereafter, the Fidelistas embarked on a terror campaign to destabilize Cuba as they detonated at least one bomb a week on the island nation; additionally, Fidel requested a foreign correspondent to accompany and document the revolution.

On February 17, 1957, *The New York Times* sent journalist Herbert Matthews to cover the war. Matthews was immediately entranced with the revolutionary; he noted that Fidel was educated, fanatical, a leader, and above all, invincible. More importantly, Matthews created for North American sympathizers and the world the legend of Fidel—the romantic figure who "dealt fairly with the peasants."[107] Matthews's writing attracted Cubans to Fidel's cause, raising the revolutionaries' morale and also lowering that of Batista's army.

Buttressed by a favorable press, an unabated bombing campaign, and a bungling Batista, Fidel's revolution grew. As the revolutionaries' terror tactics intensified—the Fidelistas bombed nightclubs, businesses, government buildings, and even schools—Batista suspended civil rights and increased arbitrary arrests, which only succeeded in driving more Cubans into Fidel's camp. Then on July 12, 1957, Fidel issued his manifesto for the movement. In essence, it called for all Cubans to form a civic revolutionary front to end Batista's oppressive rule and violation of individual rights; it also guaranteed freedom of the press and promised free elections; and it promoted a democratic government.[108]

It is important to note that in this declaration, Fidel made no mention of nationalizing public utilities or the collectivization of land. Guevara later noted that Fidel's statement was a manifesto of deception to placate the masses while he consolidated his power.[109]

Meanwhile, anarchy spread throughout Cuba: wanton arrests continue; railroads are sabotaged; fires are set in factories, warehouses, and stores; and on November 8, 1957, no less than twenty bombs detonated in Havana.[110] Cities lost electricity and water, making it difficult for the government to provide basic services. With transportation almost paralyzed, food became scarce and expensive. Batista's army was further decimated by a growing number of desertions and defections. Conversely, by this time Fidel has an effective system of maintenance and supply, for the Fidelistas are already in control of hospitals, a radio station, and even a bomb factory.[111] So on March 12, 1958, in a desperate gambit to preserve his power, Batista imposed radio and press censorship.

In response to Batista's draconian measures, the United States placed an arms embargo on the Cuban government. Enraged, Batista blamed the Yankees for his woes and declared that the US was helping the rebels by denying him arms.[112] By that time, their action was clear; by placing the embargo, the United States had lost all confidence in Batista.

Accordingly on December 17, 1958, US Ambassador Earl Smith met with Batista on instructions from the State Department to advise the Cuban ruler to resign. Batista asked if the US would intervene to stop the bloodshed, and Smith replied no.[113] Without US support, Batista decided to resign on January 1, 1959. The door was then open for Fidel and his henchmen, who seized control of Cuba.

On January 7, 1959, the United States recognized the new regime, but almost immediately, tensions rose as Fidel authorized arrests and executions. Raul Castro, the leader of the Army Division in Oriente, ordered his men to shoot one hundred prisoners without trial. Those given their day in court usually suffered the same fate. By January 20, 1959, over two hundred prisoners were executed by the Fidelistas.[114] Guevara himself admitted to ordering "several thousand" executions during the first year of Fidel's reign.[115] Many times before their execution, the condemned appallingly had up to five pints of blood extracted; many lost consciousness after the effusion of blood and had to be carried to the firing wall on stretchers. The blood was then placed in a blood bank to be shipped later to North Vietnam. Alarmed at the continuing violence, the US voiced its disapproval. Defiant, Fidel told a group of journalists that "if the U.S. did not like what was being done in Cuba they could send in the marines and then there would be 20,000 dead gringos."[116]

Fidel continued to consolidate his power base by purging political moderates he initially appointed to office, followed by issuing a decree abolishing all political parties in Cuba except his own. Additionally, Fidel declared that the promised elections would not be held for another two years; all candidates from the elections of 1954 and 1958 were banned from political life; and Raul Castro was appointed second in command should Fidel die.[117] Duplicity abounded as Fidel continued to speak of his profound populist convictions and promised the Cuban people that their standard of living would soon be raised above that of the United States.

Despite Fidel's democratic declarations, he soon planted his flag firmly in the Communist camp. When exactly Fidel became a doctrinaire Marxist was difficult to pinpoint. Before his ascension to power Fidel denounces U.S. and Soviet imperialism alike; yet, by mid-June, 1959, Castro openly endorsed Communism.[118]

Fidel's affirmation of Marxism was followed by more repression. Imprisonments, delayed trials, and executions all grew at an alarming rate. Many who supported Fidel earlier in the revolution found themselves behind bars. Tellingly, by mid-June of 1959, more people were in prison than under Batista's dictatorship,[119] and the repression continues to this day. And as in the USSR under Stalin and China under Mao, prisoners in Cuba are questioned and tortured until they deliver an acceptable self-critique, detailing their crimes against the revolution.[120] Likewise as in the Soviet gulag and the Chinese *laogai*, there were starvation diets, sleep deprivation, years in solitary confinement, and beatings, among other punishments. Presently, there are more than two hundred penal institutions in Cuba, mostly consisting of maximum-security prisons and concentration and labor camps where the incarcerated do forced labor. Apart from political dissenters, the Castro regime in particular targeted homosexuals, who were seen as an aberration of nature. The Cuban regime criminalized gay sex, and Fidel himself declared that "homosexuals should not be allowed in positions where they are able to exert influence upon young people."[121] Gays were arrested on the street for solely the way they walked or for even wearing tight pants. After their arrest, they were sent by the thousands to prison camps in the Camaguey province for intensive work[122], where they labored under the prison logo, "Work Will Make Men Out Of You."[123]

Economically, Fidel implemented his Agrarian Reform Plan, which expropriated farmlands over one thousand acres, followed by the nationalization of many American companies; on January 8, 1960, Cuba confiscated 70,000 acres of US-owned property worth 6 million.[124] In turn, the USSR agreed to buy Cuban sugar, help build factories, and supply oil.

The machinations of the Cuban dictator compels US President Dwight D. Eisenhower to declare Fidel a "madman," and in March 1960 orders the CIA to train Cuban exiles for an invasion and overthrow of Fidel's regime.[125] Eisenhower also bans the importation of Cuban sugar into the US. Not to be outdone, on July 9, 1960, over six hundred US-owned companies in Cuba are ordered by Fidel to present sworn statements disclosing their entire inventories; this action is a foreshadowing of the complete nationalization of U.S. properties in Cuba. [126]

The rising animosity between the US and Cuba was duly acknowledged by Khrushchev, who announced that the Soviets would defend Cuba with rockets if the US invaded. Che Guevara gloated that Cuba was defended by the "greatest military power in history; nuclear weapons [are] standing in the way of imperialism."[127]

Eisenhower ordered a ban on almost all US exports to Cuba; Fidel responded by seizing 382 private companies followed by the nationalization of 166 companies, including Woolworth, Sears, General Electric, International Harvester, and Coca-Cola. By the end of October 1960, U.S. investments in Cuba, valued at over 900 million, are gone.[128]

Following another vitriolic speech in which Fidel demanded the US reduced its embassy staff to eighteen—calling it a nest of spies—the US broke diplomatic relations with Cuba on January 3, 1961, propelling the two countries into decades of animosity that continues to this day.

Incensed at the incorrigible dictator, the new president John F. Kennedy implemented the plan initiated by Eisenhower to overthrow Fidel. On April 17, 1961, the poorly planned and executed Bay of Pigs invasion was launched and it failed. For Cuba, it was a tragedy because it gave Fidel another excuse to wage a campaign a terror; most of those in custody were shot, and as many as one hundred thousand were arrested. And on May 1, 1961, Fidel announced that there would never be elections in Cuba; the Cuban dictator said there was an election every day in Cuba since his regime expressed the will of the people.[129]

The Cuban people responded by voting with their feet and their flotation devices. To date, over two million have fled this version of the worker's paradise; unfortunately 80,000 have died of exposure, thirst, drowned, or were dismembered by sharks trying to reach the US.[130] Many who remained continued to pay the ultimate price: from 1960 to 1970, 14,000 Cubans were executed by the Fidelistas without due process.[131] For the Cubans that remained and survived, Fidel's promise that Cuba's economy would soon surpass that of the United States also proved illusory; food and gasoline rationing ensued along with chronic shortages of basic commodities. Before Fidel's revolution, the Cuban economy was one of the strongest in Latin America; afterward, its national income sunk to a level lower than poverty-stricken Jamaica.

And for the world, the continuance of the Castro regime proved to be deleterious as well for another confrontation. The 1962 Cuban missile crisis was the closest the world has come to a nuclear holocaust when Soviet offensive missiles were placed on Cuban soil. Robert F. Kennedy, brother to the president, spoke of sixty million Americans killed in a nuclear exchange with the Soviets; Khrushchev predicted a total of 500 million dead worldwide in a nuclear war with the United States.[132] Fortunately, the world was saved when Khrushchev backed down from Kennedy.

Unfortunately, Fidel remained in power as he exported Marxist revolution to South America, Central America, and Africa. His brother Raul remains in control of the Cuban nation today—the Fidelistas have the dubious distinction of the longest running dictatorship in the world, now running in excess of fifty-six years.

****

After that sober examination my illusions had been shattered. I could not ignore the evidence. I was questioning my allegiance to Marxist ideology. Beginning with the Bolshevik Revolution in 1917, the victims of Communist policies worldwide now approach an almost inconceivable body count of one hundred million people dead.[133] I realized that Communism is a crime of unparalleled human dimensions conjured by Karl Marx and faithfully executed by his henchmen such as Lenin, Stalin, Mao Tse-tung, Pol Pot, Fidel Castro, and others. Their goal, which calls for a classless society, where everything is shared alike, is a utopian fantasy that has never been reached despite that fact that one hundred million have died in the attempt.

But equally appalling was the revelation that I had been told nothing of the carnage during my education at Fresno State University. The progressive professors such as Bob and Beth tried the keep their classes focused on the evils of capitalism only. It took an innocent question by a classmate and my own investigation to reveal the scope of that genocide that should have been given to us as students by our professors. Where was the balance? Why were we given only one side of the story? Why was our education so slanted in one direction? In an institution that publicly proclaimed to be a bastion of diversity and critical thinking, as most institutions of higher learning claim—why was this information deliberately omitted from the classroom? That was almost as shocking as the Communist body count I had uncovered. And the answer to that would come at a later date.

In the meantime, my inquiries turned to another icon in the Leftist academic and media world, a movement that held me entranced as a child as I sat at my Abuelita's side so many years ago; it was Cesar Chavez and the Farmworker's movement.

CHAPTER 11

The Purified Cesar Chavez and the United Farmworkers' Movement: Canonized and Cropped for his Beatification

As I walked on the Fresno State University campus, I cross the Free Speech area in proximity of the Henry Madden Library. Directly north of the library is the Peace Garden. In prominent display, there are four distinctive statues: Mahatma Gandhi, Jane Addams, Martin Luther King Jr., and Cesar Chavez. It is a testament to the power and influence of these four individuals. In a university where the history and impact of countless individuals have been examined and documented the administration at Fresno State has deemed four individuals would be given the honor of statues in the garden. And the honor given to Chavez is displayed in other ways on campus. Walking through the hallways of the faculty offices of the Social Sciences Department and the Chicano-Latino Department, I see the distinctive black, red, and white flag of the United Farm Workers Union on display in front of some professors' offices, an endorsement of the accepted legacy of Chavez's most important organization.

Indeed, the prominence and reputation of Cesar Chavez is mostly beyond reproach on campus and beyond. The name of

SHATTERING THE ICONS

Cesar Chavez is given to schools, public buildings, parks, libraries, streets, and boulevards alike. Scholarships were given in his name. There is a Cesar Chavez holiday in California. The United States Postal Service produced a stamp in his honor. Deferential films and documentaries are made. President Barack Obama has designating Chavez's burial site at La Paz, in the Tehachapi Mountains, as a National Monument.[134] Murals were depicted in his image. At West Hills College in Firebaugh where I taught Chicano Studies, there is a large lecture room with a mural covering the entire side of one wall, fully twenty-five feet in length, depicting the leaders of the Chicano Movement. And in the middle of the pantheon of the esteemed heroes of *La Raza* is the largest portrait of Chavez himself: with his arms and hands extended, covering both sides of the piece and symbolically embracing all of those illustrated—like a pope giving his blessing to his flock. Ironically, among the mostly secular academic and progressive community, Chavez is a religious figure, a holy icon beyond criticism and judgment. Recently, there is even a movement to canonize him as a Catholic saint.[135] And as I researched more deeply into the life of Cesar Chavez, examining his actions as leader of the farmworker's movement, he skillfully cultivated the image of himself as a cultural Messiah, and for the most part, this propagation has worked. The purified version of Cesar Chavez is what follows in this chapter. Chavez and the UFW, through their non-violent strategies and tactics, were always on the side of the farmworker; they had only their best interests in mind; and to this day, the UFW works diligently on their behalf.

****

On the surface and at its inception, the movement was of a noble cause. Previous to the 1960s the farm workers suffered neglect and impoverished conditions at the hands of agribusiness and the conditions of the work in general. Laws were deficient—among the problems facing the migrant workers were miniscule pay for arduous work, little or no mandatory work breaks, an unsanitary or insufficient drinking water supply, no portable restrooms, and other forms of exploitation at the hands of labor contractors who took advantage of the farm workers' destitution.

Enter Cesar Chavez, whose family suffered tremendously from the Great Depression. After losing their family farm near Yuma, Arizona, the Chavez family was obligated to join the ranks of the legions of migrant family workers and traveled to California in search of work. Due to the intense competition for work, Cesar and his family rose at four in the morning and headed for the fields. Often living out of their car, over the next ten years the Chavez's harvested almost every crop California had to offer. A constant state of impermanence accompanied their odyssey as Cesar enrolled in at least thirty-six schools; finally, he had to abandon formal education after completing the eighth grade.[136]

After a two-year stint in the Navy, Chavez eventually settled in the Mexican barrio of San Jose, California, where in 1952, he met Fred Ross, a Community Service Organization (CSO) worker who mentored Chavez to register voters and organize politically. With Ross's help, Chavez assisted in establishing a CSO chapter in Oakland and also helped him realize the political results that could be gained through grass-roots activity.

Despite the political gains made on behalf of urban Chicanos in the Bay Area, Chavez felt that the CSO also needed to focus more on another neglected sector of the Chicano working class, the farm workers. Fred Ross and others disagreed. They felt that farm workers could not be organized successfully and the Chavez was striving for an unattainable goal.

Slighted, Chavez left the CSO and moved to Delano in the Southern San Joaquin Valley, the hometown of his wife Helen. It was a bold move by Chavez. With limited funds, Chavez embarked on a lengthy and time-consuming venture to organize farm workers politically. Chavez drove the length and breadth of the San Joaquin Valley, distributing questionnaires to grocery stores frequented by farm laborers, visiting them in their homes, and other activities that typically consumed a sixteen-hour workday.[137]

Despite those setbacks, the founding convention of the National Farm Workers Association (NFWA) was held in Fresno in September 1962 with Chavez as President, and Dolores Huerta, Gil Padilla, and Julio Hernandez as Vice-Presidents. The organization was later known throughout the nation and even globally as the United Farm Workers.

As noted above, the organizing process for the UFW was slow, and as Chavez and others took stock of their predicament, the consensus was that perhaps by 1968, the union would be sufficiently organized and financially solvent for an effective strike. Fate intervened, however. In the spring of 1965, Filipino workers in the Coachella Valley struck for higher wages and other concessions. The strike soon spread to the Southern San Joaquin Valley. An immediate decision faced the UFW, were they going to help the Filipinos by going on a strike as well? The UFW had only seventy dollars in its coffers, one attorney working *pro bono*, and no backing from organized labor.[138]

After much deliberation in a contentious meeting in Delano, the UFW decided to strike. It was September 16, Mexican Independence Day, and the members who were perhaps infused with a healthy dose of revolutionary fervor decided to go on a strike as well.

Now the UFW was spurred into action. In total, forty-eight ranches were struck, with picket lines covering an estimated 450 square miles of vineyards in Kern and Tulare counties.[139] Many in Delano consider the grievances raised by Chavez to be legitimate specifically in re the enforcement of state laws concerning working conditions in the fields. Nevertheless, some object to the demand by

Chavez that the growers recognize the UFW as the bargaining agent for all the field workers in the area. Another point of contention was the impact of *outsiders* on the strike. Chavez made speeches in various Bay Area colleges and universities soliciting their help. In the agitated state of the country in the 1960s, many college students heeded his call and eagerly joined the picket lines in support of the strike.

As the picket lines were drawn, the growers resorted to violence. Some drove down the edge of their property lines with spraying machines, showering the pickets with insecticide and fertilizer. Others walked up and down the picket lines, stamping on the toes of the strikers, or elbowing them on the ribs as they walked by.[140]

Resistance by the growers continued and the strike began to flounder. So in the winter of 1966, the idea of a massive farmworker's march was raised to reinvigorate the cause. The trek began in Delano, where a group of farmworkers led by Chavez began the three-hundred mile journey from Delano to Sacramento. The march garnered tremendous nationwide publicity for *la causa*, the cause, as it is now disseminated.

After two years, the union had made some gains. But its contracts, mostly with a scattering of wineries, covered only about five thousand of the state's two hundred and fifty thousand farmworkers.[141] Chavez looked to expand the strike, targeting table grape growers. So during the summer of 1967, the union implemented its most effective weapon yet—a boycott of the massive Bakersfield-based Giumarra Vineyards; it was further expanded in January 1968 to a nationwide boycott against all California table grapes.

Despite those gains, the fervor for *la causa* was waning in many areas. Morale was tottering, and some picket captains were even failing to show up at the fields. So in order to jumpstart the movement and reinvigorate his followers, in February 1968, Chavez decides on a new tactic: he goes on a fast for twenty-five days and loses more than thirty pounds in the process.[142]

Undaunted, the union continued its work. In order to put more pressure on Giumarra Farms, Chavez declared a boycott in the spring of 1969 on Safeway markets, the largest grocery chain in the west, where Giumarra sold approximately twenty percent of its grapes. Due to this added fiscal duress, and intensified by a sympathetic media featuring a cover story on the strike in *Time* Magazine, on July 29, 1970, twenty-six growers—Giumarra included—signed an agreement with Chavez's union, ending the five-year long Delano grape strike.[143]

The struggle was not over, however. The grape strike would continue up to the fall of 1973; additionally, the UFW expanded its nationwide boycott of California's non-union grapes, which included lettuce and the wines of Ernest and Julio Gallo. The protest was highlighted by another march in 1975, that time from San Francisco to Modesto, the headquarters of Gallo wine.

Another victory ensued; in 1977, after years of struggle and violence perpetuated on the UFW, the Teamsters Union officially gave up their claims to representing field workers.[144]

Formidable obstacles continued in the form of the agribusiness industry and callous growers, forcing Chavez to implement more strikes and fasts to keep *la causa* going. But through the concerted efforts, the battle was won; there were water jugs, work breaks, and portable bathrooms where none had been before. The pesticide DDT was eliminated through the efforts of the UFW. And the short-handled hoe, the bane of the field worker, was also banned. Additionally, the Agricultural Labor Relations Act was enacted, allowing farmworkers to defend themselves with the protection of a union.

Nevertheless, the decades' long battle takes the ultimate toll on the leader. On April 12, 1993, Cesar Chavez, aged sixty-six, died in his sleep. Despite the painful blow endured by his followers, the war continues to this day with his sons and extended family members, continuing to advocate and work tirelessly on behalf of the farmworkers.

****

This is where the story usually ends. When I took a class in Chicano History at Fresno State University, the above narrative was the canonical version of Cesar Chavez and the Farmworkers Movement. But there is another side to the purified Cesar Chavez story. And what follows is usually not told in the media or the classrooms of progressive academics.

CHAPTER 12

Let's Just Say we turn the Other Cheek: The Ufw, Cesar Chavez, and a Messianic Complex

As noted above, the evidence indicates that Cesar Chavez and the UFW actively cultivated the image of a cultural messiah. This is buttressed by other chroniclers of the movement: "For Chicanos, *la causa* was to become an almost religious mission, and Cesar its prophet."[145]

For example, the initial farmworker's march in 1966 from Delano to Sacramento was suggested by Chavez to have a theme: "*Perigrinacion, Penitencia,* and *Revolucion,*" meaning "Pilgrimage, Penitence, and Revolution."[146] Not coincidentally, the march took place during the Roman Catholic's holy season of Lent, and the penitents arrived in the state capital on Easter Sunday. On the way to Sacramento, prayer meetings were held at the end of each day's march, and at the head of the procession portraits of the Virgin of Guadalupe were held aloft. Others even shouldered large crosses to represent the final journey of Jesus.

When Chavez began his initial fast, many streamed to the site bearing crucifixes to pray for him. Tents were pitched for those maintaining a vigil for him, and some old women were seen crawling on their knees as they approached where Chavez was lodged, in the same manner Catholics were seen approaching the Basilica for the Virgin

Mary in Guadalupe, Mexico. And when Chavez finally broke his fast, he did it at mass where he received communion.

That was the image Chavez portrayed—the martyr dedicated to nonviolence. Yet violence was propagated within the very union he proclaimed to the world to be peaceful. Non-strikers were targeted. One woman noted, "Those of us who have resisted the union organizing efforts have been beaten, shot at, [and] deliberately run down by cars."[147] An elderly Filipino, Alfonso Pereira, got behind the wheel of his car and drove it into three growers, hitting one and breaking his hips. The Kern County Sheriff's Office discovered that Chavez supporters had purchased four thousand marbles, which they were firing with slingshots at strikebreakers into the fields. Rocks were thrown through windows in strikebreakers' homes, and one nine-year-old girl was told by a Chavez supporter that unless her father came out of the fields in support of the strike, her house would be burned to the ground.[148] Packing crates went up in flames, tires were slashed on police cars and farm trucks, and strike-breakers were roughed up by Chavez's henchmen. Three UFW supporters were arrested for shooting a Teamster organizer in Santa Maria, California.[149] Grower Carl Maggio sued the UFW and later collected more than two million dollars for damage caused by union violence.[150]

Perhaps most egregious was the UFW treatment of undocumented workers. Chavez instructed his members to call the Immigration and Naturalization Service (INS) if they suspected undocumented workers had been imported to fields targeted by the UFW. Labor camps were raided, and the undocumented were beaten near the Arizona-Mexico border. And in a dispute with citrus growers near Yuma, Arizona, the UFW called the border patrol to stop the crossing of undocumented workers. But when the INS's response was deemed too tepid by the UFW, they took matters into their own hands by beating workers as they crossed into the United States.[151]

In an attempt to consolidate Chavez's power and purge the UFW of dissenters in 1971, the union purchased a 280-acre plot of land and buildings in the Tehachapi Mountains, ironically naming it "*La Nuestra Senora de la Paz,*" or "Our Lady of Peace." Chavez moved most union operations from Delano to the site and the top administrators and their families also moved to La Paz. Now the distance from farmworkers becomes physical and their cause takes a back seat as Chavez conducted a witch-hunt at La Paz, targeting the legal department, the National Executive Board, and others by employing the methods of a drug-rehabilitation expert and noted cult leader, Charles Dietrich, to weed out the dissenters.[152]

Dietrich founded a drug rehabilitation center named Synanon, which he transformed into a group based on communal living. Dietrich declared Synanon a religion, and at the core of Synanon's practices was "The Game," a group encounter that one observer noted, "is to their religion as the Mass is to the Catholic."[153]

"The Game" is very confrontational, in which a group of people yell, curse, and scream at one targeted member for behavior deemed detrimental to the group. Dietrich encouraged Chavez to use "The Game" among union members to expose those who disagreed with his authority and thus form a new generation of like-minded sycophants. Through that exposure and subsequent purging, the UFW was less democratic as Chavez consolidated more control over the union. His actions purged a generation of talented labor leaders and replaced them with hand-picked sycophants—including most of the individuals running the UFW. For example, loyal organizer Eliseo Medina quit in 1978 after a heated argument with Chavez over changes in the legal department from which one-half of the department would be cast off in the same year. And longtime UFW attorney Jerry Cohen left in 1981 along with former Vice-President Gilbert Padilla.[154]

And the fallout continued. In the 1981 UFW convention in Fresno, the Salinas faction walked out, and its leaders were subsequently fired.[155] Long-time activist Marshall Ganz perhaps summed up the situation most succinctly: "There was no space within the Union to really be in opposition and [still] be in the Union."[156]

Three years prior to that, the union's numbers in the fields were already dwindling. At the beginning of the 1974 growing season, the UFW had fewer than a dozen growers still under contract, and less than ten thousand members.[157] These numbers continue to dwindle; in 2011, there are only about twenty-seven thousand individuals working under UFW contracts.[158] And in 2013, field workers for Gerawan Farms held a rally on front of the Agricultural Labor Relations Board office in Visalia, California, demanding that they *not* be represented by the UFW. Silvia Lopez, a fifteen-year employee of Gerawan Farms, filed a petition with the help of her attorneys. She noted, "I have friends and family who work for the companies that have the UFW. They have very bad experiences."[159] Today, most farmworkers find the UFW irrelevant. In addition, they balk at having to pay the three percent union dues demanded by the UFW. Noel Hernandez, a farmworker from Reedley, California, and two-year employee of Gerawan Farms, summed this dissenting position best by noting: "We don't need anybody representing us. They [The UFW] are going to be taking money away from us."[160]

Noel Hernandez is wise in his reluctance to support the UFW. Pilfering in the name of the farmworker is now a standard procedure for the UFW even after the death of Cesar Chavez in 1993. What has emerged from the humble beginnings of the movement is now a money-making enterprise run by the heirs of Cesar Chavez. In particular, Paul Chavez, Cesar's son, and Arturo Rodriguez, now in charge of the UFW, currently run more than a dozen tax-exempt groups that generate an estimated twenty to thirty million dollars per year.[161] Invoking Chavez's name has proven profitable for the

UFW. Public money in the form of state grants, private support, and individual donations continue to fill the coffers of the UFW. Additionally, Chavez's heirs broke with their professed solidarity with union workers and hired non-union laborers to build the three-million-dollar National Chavez Center at La Paz they now market as a tourist attraction and wedding site.[162] In 2004, tax returns show that about half of the UFW's spending—approximately 12 million dollars—goes to pay employees.[163]

In sum, the UFW has abandoned the farmworker while continuing to display the image of their icon as the farmworkers' greatest advocate. The UFW has transformed itself into a self-perpetuating organization primarily concerned with maintaining the sanitized legacy of Cesar Chavez rather than addressing the continuing problems of destitution that still plague the farmworker. The initial nominal gains made by the UFW for the farmworkers has now been superseded by the prodigious funds generated on their behalf that no longer reach them; these funds are now channeled to perpetuate the iconography of Chavez and the UFW as their benefactor and savior.

CHAPTER 13
American Leftist Professorial Hypocrisy: "I Am A Marxist"— But I Would Rather Enjoy Life In The Capitalist US

At the conclusion of my education at Fresno State University, I had some serious questions to ponder and analyze. In my experience, Fresno State was not an institution that promoted diversity of thought— through the conduct of its professors, it was rather an institution of indoctrination than education. The vast majority of the professors that I encountered were of a singular political mind and did not allow any deviation from that doctrine in their classrooms. As noted above, it was only through my own investigation that I learned that one hundred million died at the hands of Marxist ideology, ditto on my discovery of the seamier side of Cesar Chavez and the UFW. So what is going on here?

In order to fully understand the origination of these indoctrinators at Fresno State and expansively comprehend the preponderance of the American professorial world and its sympathizers in the media, one must return to the creators and their seminal work: Karl Marx, Frederick Engels, and *The Communist Manifesto*.

Although brief in length—most copies are less than ninety pages—the force it carries is almost Biblical. Published originally in February 1848, *The Communist Manifesto* delivers an apocalyptic message that presages the complete transformation of the world. Prophesized by Marx and Engels, the current world of capitalism will be overthrown by a global revolution leading to the worker—the proletariat—seizing the means of production in both industry and agriculture and leading to the withering away of the state, which will in turn usher in the classless society. In this brave new world, there will be no private property; the institution of marriage and the bourgeois family will come to an end along with other vestiges of the capitalist world. The perfectibility of man will be reached in a global communist world where strife, inequality, hunger, and war will all be eradicated, and everyone will share everything in common. In short, utopia on Earth will now become a reality.

The Communist Manifesto ends with a call to arms that will inflame the passions of anyone seeking social justice: "They [the Communists] openly declare that their ends can be attained only by the forcible overthrow of all existing conditions. Let the ruling classes tremble at a communistic revolution. The proletarians have nothing to lose but their chains. They have a world to win. WORKING MEN OF ALL COUNTRIES, UNITE!"[164]

Key to understanding this theory is Marx's declaration that his philosophy was *scientific*. Writing in the midst of the Industrial Revolution where technological and scientific discoveries flourished, Marx similarly attempted to attach the *scientific* label to his philosophy. This distinction of "Marxism as a science" is implanted in the doctrine of the Communist states his disciples found; in turn, this scientific label is accepted by the adherents of Marxism especially the Western intelligentsia would throw all semblance of objectivity out the window in their blind allegiance to this newfound doctrine.

As noted above, with the Bolshevik Revolution, Marxism germinated in Russia. Marx himself gloated, "Nowhere [else] is my success more delightful."[165] Disillusioned by the Great Depression in the 1930s and convinced that the Marxist model was the future, the Soviet Union has been forgiven of all sins in the midst of its most repressive period. Journalist Louis Fischer observed, "Lest a false impression be conveyed, it must be stated that nobody starves."[166] American writer Edmund Wilson noted, "You feel in the Soviet Union that you are at the moral top of the world."[167] Another writer, Mary Stevenson Callcott, in re the labor camps noted, "The [Soviet] authorities seek to use labor that is constructive as to character and useful economically, and not the kind that brings indignity and resentment when resorted to as punishment."[168] American labor organizer and sociologist Jerome Davis noted, "It would be in error to consider the Soviet leader [Stalin] a willful man who believes in forcing his ideas upon others."[169] The crowning statement is delivered by American Communist Tillie Olsen, who wrote in 1934 that the Soviet Union was "a heaven… brought to earth."[170]

These Old Left sycophants of the USSR go into a state of political hibernation with the signing of the Nazi-Soviet pact in August 1939; then they resuscitate their crusade when Hitler attacks the USSR in June 1941 during World War II. The political détente between the USA and the USSR ends with the conclusion of that conflict, and the Cold War which follows intensifies on the global stage.

As noted above, the USSR aids in the successful Marxist revolution in China in 1949, resulting in more repression and genocide. The Western infatuation with this latest version of the Marxist monster does not abate, however. In re the aforementioned labor camps, the co-founder of the London School of Economics, George Bernard Shaw and American journalist Anna Louise Strong both noted that Soviet and Chinese prisons were so humane and comfortable that inmates were reluctant to leave them at the termination of their sentences and that some even applied for admission.[171] Hewlett Johnson, Dean of Canterbury, saw in the murderous Mao "an inexpressible look of kindness and sympathy, an obvious preoccupation with the needs of others."[172] Harvard Sinologist John K. Fairbank noted that "the Maoist Revolution is… the best thing that happened to the Chinese people in centuries.[173] Not to be outdone, Johnson also prophesized that China is "freeing men from the bondage of the acquisitive instinct and paving the way for a new generation of life on a higher level of existence."[174]

After Mao, China falls in disfavor with most left-leaning intellectuals when Deng Xiaoping incorporates elements of capitalism into mainland China. Nevertheless, by that time, there is a new infatuation, China's progeny, the Khmer Rouge. Leftist fawning to this genocidal regime must be seen in the context of the emergence of the New Left and the Vietnam War.

****

The New Left began officially in 1962 with the Port Huron statement, authored primarily by Tom Hayden and the Students for a Democratic Society (SDS). It issued a non-ideological call for participatory democracy to be obtained by non-violent civil disobedience. The statement viewed race and the Cold War as the main problems of modern society. Despite these nonideological and non-violent proclamations, the New Left had become indistinguishable from the old by the end of the 1960s. As we have seen with the USSR, China, and other Marxist states, the transformations sought by the New Left—as envisioned by Marx—could never be obtained by peaceful means. Consequently, the non-violent integrationist policy spearheaded by Martin Luther King, Jr. in the United States was discarded for a more radical goal and agenda.

Consequently with the Vietnam War, the civil rights movement in the US mutated; violence erupted in major US cities and universities. By 1968, the SDS itself had dismissed its non-violent proclamation and was openly Marxist, and it splintered into various groups that openly advocated revolution within the United States. One of the most prominent of these was the *Weathermen* or Weather Underground led by Bill Ayers and Bernadine Dohrn, whose slogan was "Bring the War Home."[175] Accordingly in six years, the Weather Underground claimed responsibility for two dozen bombings, including the Capitol and the Pentagon in Washington, DC. These and other groups are now at war with the US and openly embrace America's totalitarian enemies.

Fanning the flames of revolution, the Vietnamese War was intensified by the media; it was the first televised war, and daily images of the conflict were broadcast nightly on the three networks. Along with draft-card burnings, campus protests, and other elements of civil unrest, the anti-war movement gained legitimacy in the eyes of the sympathetic media and by extension, was an indictment against the US and ultimately capitalism itself.

Direct US military involvement in the Vietnam War ended in August 1973. And the fall of Saigon, the capital of South Vietnam—renamed Ho Chi Minh City—in April 1975 marked an end to the war. As Communist forces consolidated their hold over Southeast Asia, the New Left celebrated the US defeat, and they believed that *social justice* would prevail in the region; in Cambodia, they believed it would be accomplished by the Khmer Rouge.

Enter esteemed Massachusetts Institute of Technology professor Noam Chomsky, author of many left-wing texts on contemporary politics and who regularly speaks to many college audiences. When reports of the atrocities committed by the Khmer Rouge emerged, Chomsky dismissed the charges as "exaggerated propaganda."[176] When the body count continued to rise, Chomsky justified the genocide by noting that it was really the fault of the United States as an "understandable response to the violence of the imperial system."[177] In this same vein, journalist Richard Dudman "did not find [in Cambodia] the grim picture painted by… refugees who couldn't take the new order." [178]

The Vietnam War had been one of the main focal points of civil unrest in the United States. Yet when the war concluded and US combat forces were sent home, Southeast Asia was no longer an interest for the Left. In the wake of the North Vietnamese victory, one hundred thousand summary executions ensued, and a million and a half boat people were driven into exile and death. Coupled with the mass murder inflicted by the Khmer Rouge, it is important to note that only after two years of Communist rule, more people had died in Southeast Asia than in the entire thirteen years of American involvement in that war.[179] But that fact nary raised an eyebrow from the Left: genocide under Communist rule was of no concern to them.

We now turn from Southeast Asia to Cuba, where North American progressive bootlicking continued for Fidel and his ilk. When Fidel's caravan entered Havana only days after their victory, Nancie Matthews, Herbert Matthews's wife, swooned at the sight of the revolutionary: "It is all like the Second Coming of Christ—beard and all.[180] To journalist Saul Landau, Fidel was "steeped in democracy," to American professor Leo Huberman, Castro was "a passionate humanitarian."[181] Writer Norman Mailer thought Fidel was "the first and greatest hero to appear in the world since the Second World War;" and American social activist Abbie Hoffman noted that when Fidel stood erect, "he is like a mighty penis coming to life, and when he is tall and straight, the crowd immediately is transformed."[182]

Equally, Che Guevara held the progressives entranced. Before his death, he was reputed to be "the most idealistic, self-denying, and puritanical of the Cuban leaders."[183] His supposed disdain for the trappings of material comfort were buttressed by academic Ariel Dorfman, who noted, "Nothing could be more vicariously gratifying than Che's disdain for material comfort and everyday desires."[184] Professor Maurice Zeitlin declared, "No social justice is possible without a vision like Che's."[185] Fidel himself contributed to the accolades when at the dedication to Che's mausoleum in Cuba, he said, "His luminous gaze of a prophet has become a symbol for all the poor of the world."[186]

****

As noted above, the Leftist academic declares that Marxism is science. This idea leads to many unfortunate consequences mainly that the individuals professing it feel that they have discovered the unalterable truth, and therefore any evidence to the contrary must be in error or a mere aberration on the path toward justice and peace.

Secondly, the orthodox Marxist heaps scorn on religion, claiming it to be the "opium of the people." Nevertheless, upon further inquiry, Marxism is not science—it is a religion. Marxism merely supplants one religious belief for another. And as such, it demands unwavering devotion by its academic disciples. Like other monotheistic faiths, Marxism makes the grandiose proclamation that utopia can be constructed on Earth. While the monotheist claims the intervention of God is needed to achieve that goal, the Marxist claims utopia will be reached by eradicating capitalism; and following that eradication, human perfectibility will be achieved. So in order to achieve that noble goal, all types of human engineering is justified. This justification is concisely noted by Robert Conquest: "1) There is much injustice under Capitalism; 2) Socialism will end this injustice; 3) Therefore anything that furthers Socialism is to be supported; 4) including any amount of injustice."[187]

Additionally, the victims are dehumanized. A Soviet party official told resisting peasants, "Karl Marx, our dear dead leader, wrote that 'peasants are potatoes in a sack.' We have got you in our sack."[188] Former Soviet party member Lev Kopelev noted: "We were raised as the fanatical adepts of a new creed, the only true *religion* of scientific socialism. The party became our church militant, bequeathing to all mankind eternal salvation, eternal peace and the bliss of an earthly paradise.... The works of Marx, Engels and Lenin were accepted as holy writ, and Stalin was the infallible high priest."[189]

So anyone who resists is an obstacle to *eternal salvation* and needs to be eliminated. They are classified not as people but *enemies of the people* or labeled as *reactionaries*. Class enemies like the kulaks are dehumanized into *counter-revolutionaries*, in the same manner that Hitler dehumanized the Jews.

And if the people fail to believe in the cause, we have seen that force is necessary for their lack of vision and progress. This argument becomes supremely ironic for as Collier and Horowitz noted, "The Idea of 'the people' is more important than the people themselves."[190] Consequently, because of this blind faith, Marxist genocides are merely *errors* or *mistakes*. There is no inquiry as to whether the faith itself must be in error.

Moreover, Marx and the Communist leadership that followed secluded themselves from the very people they claimed to represent. Marx himself spent many years in libraries and his own study. There is no evidence that Marx actually talked to peasants and landowners. And there is no evidence that Marx ever entered a factory or mine, or any other industrial workplace his entire life.[191] Similarly with Lenin, who also never visited a factory or set foot on a farm. Nor was Lenin ever seen amongst the working class in any town in which he lived.[192] According to Khrushchev, Stalin also separated himself from the masses, and his last visit to a village was in 1928.[193] Soviet Intelligence Officer Walter Krivitsky, like many Communist elites, resided in luxury while his countrymen starved during the famine. He justified this by noting, "We are traveling a difficult road to socialism... We must eat well and relax after our labors... for it is we who are building the happy life of the future."[194] Similarly in China, most of the privileged Communist Party officials suffered least. Like Mao, they had ample access to the grain reserves, and they lived in separate compounds from the peasantry. Pol Pot never labored on a farm either. Despite his professed egalitarianism, Che Guevara justified Marxist leadership thus: "Revolutionary institutions... permit the natural selection of those who are destined to march in the vanguard, and who dispense rewards and punishments to those who fulfill their duty or act against the society under construction."[195] After the Cuban revolution, Che did not need to construct anything for his comfort; he established his residence on Tarara Beach, fifteen miles from Havana, in a mansion with seven bathrooms, a sauna, a massage salon and a swimming pool with a waterfall, among other amenities.[196] And then there is the account given by Juan Reinaldo Sanchez, Fidel's personal bodyguard for over seventeen years. As Sanchez notes, Fidel's pledged egalitarianism is also a ruse. Fidel's assets include a 90-foot luxury yacht, a two-story mansion with a swimming pool on a 75 acre estate on his own private island, maintained with the labor of domestic servants.[197] This luxury residence is only one of at least twenty other houses owned by Fidel. Sanchez's assertion of Fidel's opulent lifestyle is buttressed by an article in *Forbes* magazine, which in 2006 tallied the riches of the fortunes of royalty and dictators globally. In *Forbes*'s estimation, they placed Fidel's wealth at approximately $900 million, placing him in the top ten, despite Fidel's claim that his only possession was his monthly salary of 900 pesos.[198]

****

SHATTERING THE ICONS

This detachment from the people demonstrated by Communist leaders can be seen in the American Leftist academic world as well. Insulated in their scholastic community from their bully pulpit, they castigate a vulgar capitalist culture seeped in poverty, unemployment, violence, crass commercialism, and crude commercial transactions. Yet it is this same crude society that gives them financial support so that they can continue to berate it. Because of their estrangement from this society—like my Abuelita—they vainly seek a cure in another type of government. Consequently they give *carte blanche* to totalitarian regimes. This attitude is best noted by Marxist philosopher Georg Lukas, who said, "I have always thought that the worst form of socialism is better to live in than the best form of capitalism.[199]

Despite their vehemence toward capitalism, many Marxist academics prefer to live in non-Marxist nations. I witnessed this hypocrisy myself. In a small graduate seminar, I and about ten of my classmates visited our professor at his home for an informal meeting and party. He and his wife lived in an upper-middle-class gated community in a very large house with a swimming pool and other amenities. After dinner and an ample amount of liquor, disclosures ensued, and I also learned that he had a housekeeper and landscaper to maintain his large domicile. Obviously, he and his wife lived a very comfortable lifestyle. Then while we were all in his living room discussing politics, he looked around the gathered and declared to us proudly, "I am a Marxist."

My classmates, most already numbed by alcohol, merely nodded in agreement. I had also imbibed, and in deference to our generous host and professor, I also nodded in silence. Yet my mind was racing. At that point, I was in the final stages of shedding my Marxist upbringing; the proud proclamation by my professor finally put me over the top.

Going home, I ruminated over his professed Marxism *vis-à-vis* his lifestyle. He owned a beautiful home, private property. He was married, also a bourgeois institution. He employed a housekeeper and landscaper—he subjugated workers to wage labor. What hypocrisy! My professor's lifestyle was in direct opposition to his professed Marxism. And he is not alone. I suspect most of the well-salaried Left-leaning professors I encountered at Fresno State and throughout the United States live approximately the same lifestyle; ironically, the very lifestyle they continue to scorn in their writings and lectures. Those academics remind me of the elite Communist leaders noted above. They also lived comfortable lives apart from the proletariat, the very people they claimed to represent. It was the same with Cesar Chavez and the UFW leaders; by moving to La Paz, they also distanced themselves physically, mentally, and financially from the farmworkers they claimed to represent.

****

It is these discoveries that set me on a new path. I discovered their slavish devotion to Marxism superseded any attempt at objectivity in the classroom. To question these so-called advocates of diversity, to say perhaps that there are some beneficial elements to capitalism and can we discuss them in class would not be entertained because it would be analogous to saying to the preacher that perhaps Satan had some good qualities and can we discuss them in church. The preacher could not accept it because it would deny his faith. Likewise, many of the professors I encountered could not accept it either because it would deny their faith because it is this dogmatic blueprint that must be followed at all cost. If these academics were to acknowledge that the supposed agents of social evolution and the ideology they implement actually hurt the people they purport to protect, then the faith, the ideal, and the Marxist goal would now be exposed as fraudulent. And so it is a faith they cannot deny because it is their religion. To deny that faith is heretical, and that is something that they cannot acknowledge.

Consequently from what I witnessed in the classroom firsthand, *the ends justify the means*. To these academics, it doesn't matter how many lives are displaced, how many people are sent to labor in the Mephistophelean gulag, and how many kulaks starve and cook their children; it doesn't matter how many mountains of corpses are piled up if the idea, the religion, of the perfect and just society is the end goal. So they turn a blind eye. So they dismiss. They deny, they excuse, and they do anything but admit Communism was wrong because that is *their faith*, and therefore, damn it, their students should believe it too because it is *the truth*.

Class after class, semester after semester, I was subjected to that. Blinded by their dogma, those teachers were not educators; they were indoctrinators. Beth demonstrated that domestics showed deference to their employers—so what? Bob showed us that a woman who could not get ice cream for her children after her welfare funds ran out was someone who should be worthy of our sympathy and collective tears—so what? And as I sat in class and ruminated over these trivialities, the banal demonstrations of *inequality* while through my own work, I discovered an unacknowledged and ignored one hundred million dead, a life-changing thought began to germinate in my consciousness, "I can teach better than these professors. I can educate, not indoctrinate." And that was when I decided to become a college professor.

PART III
My Students: The Good, the Bad, and the Not-So-Pretty

CHAPTER 14

Critical Thinking in the Classroom: To Bomb or Not to Bomb, That is the Question

Of course, all instructors and students have biases. As noted above, what I witnessed in the classroom as a student was a calculated effort on the part of most of my instructors to persuade their students to think in a certain way. As I witnessed and experienced this, it became apparent to me that in an institution of higher learning like Fresno State University, an effort to at least try and implement a diversity of thought was lacking.

So when I began to teach at West Hills College, the Madera Center, and Clovis Community College, one of the first things I do at the start of each semester is to introduce my students to my methodology of instruction.

Under the rubric of "problems in history" I write on the board this date: "Dec. 7, 1941." I do this for all my classes for a simple reason; it is a recognizable date for most students. Even if many students are lacking a significant historical foundation, most know what happened on that date—some even have a grandfather or acquaintance who was in World War II and this makes it more germane.

So with this written on the board, I ask the class, "What happened on this date?"

Many hands go up and someone answers, "The Japanese attacked Pearl Harbor."

With that, I proceed to go through a brief synopsis of the attack. "That is correct. Six Japanese aircraft carriers launch a two-wave aerial attack approximately 220 miles northwest of the island of Oahu on Pearl Harbor and other military installations on that island. The attack, mainly consisting of 350 planes, including dive bombers, high-level bombers, fighter planes, and torpedo planes, inflict significant damage to the United States Pacific fleet and Army Air Corps forces stationed there. Approximately 3,580 Americans are killed, wounded or missing, 18 major vessels are damaged, over two hundred aircraft are destroyed or damaged, and this triggered the United States' entry into the Second World War… That is the abridged version, yes?"

Rows of heads nod in approval.

"OK, if we can all agree that these were the basic facts of the attack, what about interpretation? Facts cannot be seen in a vacuum. The human mind usually tries to make sense about what we experience, and historical phenomena are not an exception to that rule."

By this time, I see some puzzled looks and then I proceed, "OK, if you were to ask an American veteran who was at Pearl Harbor and who witnessed and survived the attack, what would he say about the nature of the attack, and the Japanese in particular?"

A student will usually reply that the American GI would be angry about the attack.

Then I prod them further. "OK, why would he be angry about the attack? At what time did the attack take place? The first alarm was raised a few minutes before 8:00 a.m. Additionally, the attack was executed on a Sunday morning. Why did they attack on a Sunday morning? The answer was obvious. The Japanese clearly wanted to surprise the Americans at Pearl Harbor, and they did. Most American servicemen were asleep and woefully unprepared for the attack on that fateful Sunday morning.

"So of course any American servicemen would be angry. If you read the eyewitness accounts of the survivors, many were in Honolulu or Waikiki the night before, dancing with their dates, quaffing beer with their buddies, and having a great time. Then the next morning, all hell suddenly breaks loose and many of their friends are now dead. What galls the GI even more is that the Japanese shun protocol and do not declare war beforehand. It was a bona fide sneak attack. Even today, after more than seventy years to ruminate on the event, many American veterans have not forgiven the Japanese. Many still refer to them as 'those dirty Japs."

At this point in my narration, most students are in agreement; many have heard of this American interpretation previously. But now I present another version.

"OK, now suppose you are a Japanese war veteran or Japanese citizen living in Japan who lived during the Pearl Harbor attack. What do you think their rendition of the attack would be?"

Usually, there is silence. So I have to coax them a bit more. "To the Japanese, US President Franklin Delano Roosevelt did something in 1940 that triggered the attack, what do you think that was?"

Occasionally, a sagacious student will deliver the correct answer, but this is usually not the case, so I continue: "In 1940, in order to stop Japanese aggression into mainland Asia, FDR cut off the supply of raw materials, (i.e., gasoline and scrap metal that the Japanese were using to expand their empire). So from the Japanese point of view, this economic embargo initiated by the United States is an overt act of aggression. Consequently, the Japanese view is that they were *forced* to attack the United States, to demoralize them, and bring them back to the negotiating table to reopen commerce once again so that the Japanese can continue their expansion unfettered by

American interference. So from the Japanese perspective, their attack on Pearl Harbor was really our fault."

This account is usually met with stunned silence followed by many quizzical looks. They have not been subjected to this type of critical thinking.

With their attention firmly in hand, I then shift into another gear. Next, I write on board the Japanese cities of Hiroshima and Nagasaki. "OK, who knows what happened to these cities near the end of World War II?"

Almost everyone's hands shoot into the air. Like Pearl Harbor, it is a well-known event.

Someone answers, "The United States dropped two atomic bombs on those cities."

"Correct, on August 6, 1945, a United States B-29 Superfortress bomber dropped an atomic bomb on Hiroshima. This was followed by another detonation of an atomic weapon, this time on the city of Nagasaki, three days later. And what do you expect the Japanese think of these events?"

I already know the answer to this question. The usual response from my students is typically the same as the Japanese point of view, and what they have been taught by most professors and the media. The atomic bombs have been depicted as an unnecessary weapon—a terrorist weapon—resulting in the extermination of the Japanese who had already given up on the war. And admittedly, there is a lot of evidence to support this perception. To augment this point of view, I mention that I have been to Hiroshima and have visited the memorial museum there.

"In this museum, there are graphic displays of the carnage heaped upon the Japanese by the American atomic bomb dropped in that city. There is a slab of concrete from a bridge where the shadows of Japanese victims have been burned into it. There are photographs of Japanese women where the floral pattern on their kimonos have been branded into their skin. There are images of Japanese children whose skin have melted from their faces, exposed to the bone. There are accounts of the water reservoirs in Hiroshima boiling because of the intensity of the heat. Planted potatoes were baked underground. Some Japanese women were so traumatized by the bombing that they carried their dead babies in their arms for days. And of the 245,000 people in Hiroshima, approximately 100,000 died that day, and thousands died subsequently.[200] "In Nagasaki, the Japanese suffered similarly. There, about 75,000 Japanese died on August 9, 1945, and of course thousands later succumbed due to the residual atomic radiation.[201]

"So you can see why the Japanese saw the atomic bombs as a needless destruction of innocent lives, an unnecessary weapon detonated upon an enemy that was about to give up. Indeed, they see the dropping of the bombs as not only a criminal act but ultimately, as an act against humanity itself."

At this point, most students are nodding in agreement—no disagreement yet.

"OK, that is the Japanese' point of view. Now, what about the other side of the coin?"

By their collective puzzled looks, I can deduce what is firing in their craniums—"There is another point of view on this?"

"OK, let's look at the latter stages of the Pacific war. After a shattering defeat for the Japanese in the Battle of Midway in June 1942, they are fighting a defensive war. And as the American forces are approaching Japan, what is happening to Japanese resistance, is it increasing or decreasing?"

Not surprisingly, many students believe that Japanese resistance was diminishing.

"No, Japanese opposition to American advancement is significantly *increasing*. For example, let's look at the Battle of Guadalcanal beginning in August 1942, the Japanese lose 25,000 men. Similarly at

Tarawa Atoll in November 1943, the Japanese lose almost their entire force of 5,000 men. Following that at Kwajalein, 8,500 Japanese die, decimating almost their entire force.[202]

"And the carnage continues. Beginning in February 1945 at Iwo Jima, the 21,000 Japanese defenders die almost to a man. Only a few hundred wounded Japanese survive to become prisoners of war.[203] Not surprisingly, American casualties are also increasing.

"With American forces ominously approaching the Japanese main islands, Japanese desperation intensifies. At Saipan, the increasing Japanese military casualties are augmented by the mass suicides of thousands of civilians, mostly women and children. American soldiers are mortified when they witness civilians gather at the northern tip of the island and hurl themselves over the cliffs onto the jagged rocks below.

"More desperation ensues. In the Battle of Leyte Gulf in late 1944, for the first time, the Japanese are using in large numbers kamikaze pilots. Kamikaze means 'divine wind,' and refers to the typhoon which destroyed most of the massive invasion fleet of the Mongol Emperor Kublai Khan in the thirteenth century. The same type of mentality pervades here. The Japanese are facing the first full-scale invasion of their home islands in over six hundred years, this time by American forces. The kamikaze are now called to repel the invader as was done hundreds of years ago.

"And most of the pilots go willingly to their death. Many are college-educated Japanese who see it as an honor to die for their country because they believe when they sacrifice themselves, their spirits will reside at the celebrated Shrine of the Righteous Souls, at *Yasukuni*, near the Imperial Palace in Tokyo, where even the Emperor will bow in their honor. Some even go to their own funeral before taking off in a bomb-laden aircraft, and their task is simple, find the largest American ship, crash their plane into it, and kill themselves and as many of these barbarians as possible to prevent the invasion of the sacred Japanese islands.

"Why are they doing this? Because most of the Japanese at that time believed in the concept of *Yamato-damashii*, which translates roughly into the 'Japanese fighting spirit.' This encompasses the idea that the Japanese are a special people, racially pure, and culturally superior to the rest of the world, and this must be defended at all costs. To the Japanese, their culture and family are everything, and if necessary, everything must be sacrificed to defend it.

"Now, let's look at the momentous battle of Okinawa only 350 miles south of the main Japanese island of Kyushu. Here, the Japanese are especially fortified, having constructed sixty miles of interconnected and multi-leveled tunnels, some four stories in depth.[204] A United States Naval bombardment is not going to dislodge the Japanese. The only way the Americans are going to defeat the Japanese entrenched in Okinawa is through brutal, close-quarter, yard-by-yard combat. On Sugarloaf Hill, part of the main western Japanese defense on the island, the United States Marine Corps fight perhaps the most intense tactical battle in their storied history. The Marines capture Sugarloaf Hill twelve times—and twelve times they are driven off by the fanatical Japanese. Finally on the thirteenth try the Marines capture the hill—but at significant cost. The Marines suffer almost three thousand killed and seriously wounded: a ghastly price to pay for a hill measuring only fifty feet high and three hundred yards long.[205]

"Previous to this on the high seas, the Japanese concoct a scheme to dispatch their only remaining operational battleship the *Yamato* to Okinawa on a kamikaze mission of its own. With minimal escort and no air cover, the plan calls for the *Yamato* to steam toward the island, breach the massive US fleet deployed around Okinawa, deliberately ground the famed battleship on the shore, and using its massive guns as cover, have the sailors disembark to reinforce the Japanese defenders there. Of course the plan is doomed to failure. Most of the Japanese who took part in this mission knew that since the *Yamato* carried no lifeboats or rafts. But better to have the *Yamato* go down in a blaze of glory than remain shamefully anchored in Japanese waters to be surrendered intact to Allied forces. So the plan is executed and the result is never in doubt. US submarines detect the Japanese force off the coast of Kyushu and US carrier-borne aircraft are dispatched to dispose of the massive battleship. On April 7, 1945, the battleship *Yamato* sinks about one hundred miles off the Kyushu coast after taking at least eleven torpedoes and eight heavy bombs; after sinking to the bottom of the sea with 3,063 Japanese sailors and officers, only 269 survive.[206] "So the campaign in Okinawa ends on June 21, 1945, after eighty-two days of horrific combat. The Japanese lose Okinawa and by some accounts up to 185,000 killed. The Americans also suffer their highest casualties from the Pacific war with 12,520 dead or missing.[207]

"Additionally, the Japanese main islands are also taking a thrashing by newly-deployed B-29s. From March to July 1945, B-29s, using primarily napalm cluster incendiaries, drop 100,000 tons of bombs on sixty-six Japanese cities and towns, wiping out 170,000 square miles of densely-populated areas. On the night of March 9, 1945, over three hundred B-29s ignited Tokyo into a blazing inferno, leveling fifteen square miles of the city, killing over 80,000 and injuring over 100,000. The Japanese calculated that American bombing raids on sixty-nine areas destroyed over two million buildings, leaving nine million homeless, and killed 260,000 and injuring 412,000.[208]

"Still, the Japanese continue to resist. One Kamikaze pilot wrote, 'All Japanese must become soldiers and die for the Emperor'.[209] Reflecting this view, on June 6, 1945, the Japanese Supreme Council approve a document which noted, 'we shall prosecute the war to the bitter end.' The document also includes the final plan for the defense of Japan, including 10,000 kamikaze pilots, fifty-three infantry divisions, and twenty-five brigades. It also calls for a civilian militia of 28 million, utilizing weapons such as bamboo spears and bows and arrows.[210] Schoolchildren in Japan are practicing for the American invasion by strapping satchels to their chests and running and diving on their stomachs to simulate a suicide bombing attack under an American tank.

"Meanwhile, the Americans are also preparing for the invasion of Japan, Operation Downfall, and the plan of action is quite grim. Divided into two sections, the first phase, Operation Olympic, is slated to commence in late 1945, the assault on Kyushu. This is to be followed in March 1946 by Operation Coronet, the attack on Honshu. But most of Kyushu is mountainous like Okinawa, providing excellent terrain for defensive warfare. Additionally, the Japanese have moved thirteen divisions into Kyushu for the defense of that island. Because of these developments, US General Douglas MacArthur estimated a total of one million American casualties for the invasions of Kyushu and Honshu alone.[211]

"In the meantime, US President Harry S. Truman is notified of the first successful detonation of the atomic bomb in Alamogordo, New Mexico on July 16, 1945. Of course, Truman is aware of the mounting casualties in the Pacific war and in particular Okinawa and knows of General MacArthur's dire American casualty predictions of a non-atomic invasion of Japan. Do you think now Truman is going to hesitate to use the bomb?"

The students who were convinced that dropping the atomic bombs on Japan was a criminal act are now thinking otherwise. I can see it in their faces.

"Put yourselves in President Truman's shoes. The United States has spent 2 billion dollars and employed over 120,000 people, working at thirty-seven different facilities in nineteen states to build the atomic bomb. Of course, Truman is not going to hesitate. In his own words, he wanted to use the atomic bomb to administer a 'tremendous shock' to the Japanese and convince them that the United States had the power 'to destroy the Empire'.[212] Others concur. George M. Elsey, a Naval Intelligence officer in Washington noted, 'Truman made no decision because there was no decision to be made. He could no more have stopped it than a train moving down a track'.[213] But for argument's sake, let's say that Truman does not tell the American people we have an atomic bomb, decides not to use it on the Japanese, and the Americans proceed with a non-atomic invasion of Japan with only half of the casualties as projected by MacArthur. Would Truman have been seen as a humanitarian by the American people?

"No, because the atomic bomb could not be kept a secret forever. Because of the legions of individuals employed and the many institutions in which research was done, eventually, someone was going to reveal to the public that we had this *super weapon* that could have ended the war quickly, and we didn't use it. There was so much pressure on Truman to use the atomic bomb on the Japanese to end the war. I sincerely think he never really considered not using it. I am convinced Truman feared incalculable political and personal repercussions when the existence of this super weapon was in the hands of the Americans was revealed and we did not use it. So from Truman's and Elsey's perspective, the President had no choice, he had to use the bomb.

"So as I said before, the first atomic bomb is dropped on Hiroshima with the resulting deaths. But still, the Japanese are not ready to give up. In fact, what most people do not realize is that the Japanese are also working on building their own atomic bomb. After Hiroshima, the Japanese government summons their leading physicist, Yoshio Nishina, to Tokyo to ask if the atomic detonation was authentic, and whether he could duplicate it in a matter of months.[214] So a single American atomic detonation on the Japanese did not change their mindset.

"Consequently three days later, a second atomic bomb is dropped on Nagasaki, thousands more die, and still, the Japanese government is bickering. The final decision to surrender does not take place until five days after this second bomb is dropped. The War Minister and the two Chiefs of Staff opposed it. Emperor Hirohito intervenes and records a message of surrender to the Japanese people. Japanese Army officers break into the Imperial Palace to destroy the recording before it is broadcast, killing the head of the Imperial Guard in the process. But they fail to stop the broadcast, and immediately after the communication, the War Minister and others commit suicide in the Imperial Palace.[215]

"So this weapon of mass destruction is used on the Japanese and is forever etched in their minds and history. Most Japanese will not budge in noting the excessive, destructive force and criminality of its application. For the Americans, however, the bomb finally produces the intended result. The Japanese surrender and the war ends. And taking into account the intensity of Japanese resistance as US forces approach Japan, this fanaticism compels the Americans to use the atomic bombs to save American lives. President Truman justifies using this weapon because he 'hoped that there was a possibility of preventing an Okinawa from one end of Japan to the other.'[216] American survivors of Okinawa see the atomic bombs not as a criminal act but rather as a weapon that saved their lives. One wounded veteran of that campaign wrote: 'When the bombs dropped and the news began to circulate that "Operation Olympic" would not, after all, take place... we cried with relief and joy. We were going to live. We were going to grow up to adulthood after all'.[217] For the Americans, the detonation of the atomic bombs on the Japanese is almost seen as an act of mercy because Allied commanders estimated that Japanese casualties of a non-atomic invasion of Japan would be in the range of 10 to 20 million.[218] So for the Americans, the atomic bombs not only saved American lives—the *bombs saved Japanese lives.*

"Now, you propose this argument to the Japanese that the bombs were actually an act of mercy, and they saved Japanese lives, what do you think they will say? Of course, they will question your sanity especially after a trip to the museum in Hiroshima. You can understand their point of view. So in this case, I have presented you with a historical event with two different points of view and keep in mind that there are more. So here is the crux of the matter, who is correct?"

By this time, there is abject silence in the classroom not out of boredom but from collective contemplation. They are not sure what to answer now. And the reason is that most of them have not been subjected to this type of reasoning in the classroom. They have been indoctrinated, not educated.

Many times, after this collective contemplation, I receive this response, "Well, what do you think, Mr. Luna?"

That is not what I want to hear.

"*It doesn't matter what I think.* That is not my job. My job is not to spoon-feed you my opinion and state it as fact. My task is to provide you with the historical information as objectively as possible and then have you make your own interpretation for that particular event. And it is my fervent hope you will go home, contemplate this exercise, and conjure up a new interpretation about this very controversial event."

****

That is a new exercise for many students, lines of reasoning that most of them have yet to take. But to further enhance the classroom experience, it is important to also engage the students in other ways for many of them also have important stories to tell. What follows are some of the more interesting, amusing, and tragic events in my teaching experience.

CHAPTER 15

In Country: Bill and Patrick's Not-So-Excellent Combat Adventures in Vietnam

A pertinent example of enhancing the classroom experience by utilizing students came from my time as an instructor at West Hills College. There I met a seasoned individual named Bill, who took two classes from me. Bill was a tall, strapping, and gregarious man with a merry laugh and an ample girth to match. He reminded me of Santa Claus without the beard.

At that time, I was teaching Colonial and Modern United States history classes in succession, and since Bill was enrolled in both, we then had a chance to chat between classes. Since Bill was not the typical eighteen-year-old college student, I decided to pick his brain, and he then gave me an account of his life, particularly in the military as an Air Force Officer in the Vietnam War. His tale was so intriguing that I felt compelled to set aside time to allow him to tell his tale in class.

Bill was a pilot of a C-47 military transport plane flying out of Da Nang in South Vietnam. Once as he was approaching take-off speed on the runway, his plane was hit by a rocket-propelled grenade—the explosion consumed the aircraft. Bill remembered taking shrapnel and the plane crashing, but after that, he was rendered unconscious. When the plane was engulfed in flames someone—and Bill still doesn't know who—broke through the pilot's window and pulled him from the aircraft, saving his life. Bill was the only survivor in the aircraft; the rest of his crew members died in the attack.

As Bill recounted his tale to the class, they sat transfixed. The students peppered him with questions afterward, and he and the students were visibly affected by his account. Because the Vietnam War was still controversial, Bill's story produced the desired effect. I could deliver a lecture on the conflict, but there was nothing like having a veteran in class who experienced it and was not reluctant to give his side of the story. When Bill finished, the students were provided with an insight that I could never deliver.

Bill ended his tale with a penetrating anecdote. One of the physical problems that affect him to this day is the shrapnel still lodged in his body. Bill told the class that even at the moment with the war on terror and heightened airport security, he had difficulty going through detectors because they invariably picked up the metal in his body. Consequently, the former Air Force pilot detested flying commercially because after he went through a detector and a body search, he still triggered an alarm, so he had to tell airport officials of his Vietnam mission mishap. And periodically while drying himself off after a shower, he heard the metal clink as it hit the floor. Forty years on, Bill's body was still expurgating itself of the shrapnel from that fateful attack. Shedding metal used to alarm him, but at present, Bill said he just laughed and took in all in stride. My students, however, were collectively thunderstruck and just shook their heads in wide-eyed amazement as he recounted his tale.

****

Another Vietnam vet contributed greatly to my class as well, but his story was initially more difficult to extricate. Patrick enrolled in my class at the old Clovis Community College Center on Herndon Avenue. A stout Hispanic with a massive muscle-bound frame, a full wolfmanlike mane of hair, Fu Manchu moustache, and wide unblinking, piercing eyes, Patrick was not easy to forget. Sitting front and center, his unobstructed and penetrating stare measured my every move. His countenance conveyed a man on the edge; occasionally during a lecture, I would see his eyes bulge and his face turn crimson, valiantly trying to suppress an opinion to my lecture like a layer of hot pulsating magma pushing to explode on the surface. But he managed to keep the eruption at bay. Because of his intensity, I was initially very reluctant to call upon him in class. I had no idea how he would respond. Nevertheless, I decided to try and get some more information on him before I did anything rash. During the student introductions at the beginning of the semester, I knew he was a Vietnam War veteran, but that was about it. Then like the hippie woman in Bob's class, I ascertained some measure of his personality by his attire. I noticed occasionally he wore T-shirts adorned with American flags, bald eagles, and "Remember Vietnam MIA's" emblazoned across his barrel chest. From that, I knew that he was proud of his military service, and so I decided to get him to tell his tale to the class. Occasionally after a session, I carefully approached him and urged him to give his account to his classmates.

"Mr. Luna, I can't do that. You are the teacher," Patrick replied.

Instinctively, I knew Patrick had a dynamic story to tell, but he needed some prodding. Racking my brains, I decided to show a documentary on the Vietnam War. The film was blatantly one-sided. Graphic combat footage depicted American tanks spewing arcs of fire into buildings, carpet-bombing B-52s opening their bellies and releasing tons of ordinance, raining death on the unfortunate below, and murderous machine gun firing collectively portrayed US forces as slaughtering civilians indiscriminately. In contrast, interviews with the North Vietnamese Army and Viet Cong portrayed them as noble and heroic, stoically trying to repel the American genocidal invaders.

As the film progressed, I saw the veteran's agitation level increase measurably. Patrick squirmed in his chair, rubbed his hands through his beard and hair, tapped his pencil on the desk loudly—all signs that the magma layer was about to break to the surface. And when the film ended and the class was dismissed, he deliberately stayed for a personal talk.

"What's on your mind?" I asked.

Patrick's face approached within one foot of mine, his eyes aflame, and he retorted, "I almost walked out in the middle of that film."

"Why?"

"Damn it, Mr. Luna, that film is *completely* biased," he fumed, approaching me even closer, his hot breath cooling the beads of sweat forming on my upper lip.

"Well, you were there. Would you now like to talk about your experience in Vietnam?"

"You mean to you?"

"No, I mean to the class. I can set aside some class time, and you can give an account of your experience there."

Patrick's fury subsided and transformed into determination: "OK, I will do it."

The following week, I turned the lectern over to Patrick. He began with some prepared notes but soon began to speak extemporaneously.

"I want to thank Mr. Luna for giving me this time to speak to you about my experience in Vietnam. I was a combat Marine and saw a lot of action," he began.

"That video showed the Americans in a bad light. I know that civilians were killed in 'Nam. But this was not a typical war, like World War II. The Viet Cong did not wear uniforms like a soldier.

They would attack us then blend into the civilian population. So how could we attack an enemy like that? It was practically impossible to root them out without civilian casualties.

"We also fought in the jungle—it was full of booby-traps. On the jungle trails, Charlie dug pits with bamboo spikes on the bottom, camouflaged on top. The bamboo pits could not be detected until you stepped and fell into it. The Viet Cong also buried bullets vertically, attaching a nail to the firing pin. So any pressure from the top would fire the round, most likely into a foot. It wasn't going to kill you, but it sure hurt like hell. Charlie also used trip wires attached to a grenade in a tin can that was hanging from a tree. The grenade already had its firing pin pulled. So anyone passing underneath the tree would trip the wire, pulling the grenade from the can, exploding it. So you can see, just walking in the jungle could maim you or even be fatal.

"We didn't get any rest at night either. When we were in country and in our foxholes, Charlie liked to ambush us at night, so we had to be constantly on the watch. We would go days without adequate sleep, waiting for the next attack. Some of my fellow Marines who dozed on watch paid the price—they had their throats cut by the Viet Cong."

Patrick's voice was cracking by then and his hands, holding his prepared notes, began to shake violently.

"All that was bad enough, but how we were treated coming back home was in many ways worse. Protestors gathered on the Golden Gate Bridge and spat upon troops coming home as they sailed underneath. How do you like that for a 'welcome home?'

"And adjusting to civilian life? That took years. When I first came back home and slept in my own bed with my wife, she too became a victim. Because in the morning when I was not fully conscious, I would have flashbacks that I was back in that goddamn foxhole in 'Nam. I would feel something stir beside me and thought it was another ambush by Charlie. So almost by instinct, I would grab my wife's throat, choking her, thinking it was the Viet Cong. I almost killed her a couple of times before I fully woke up and realized what I was doing. She wised up though. In the early morning, she trained herself to rise before I did. Then she went to a corner of the bedroom, out of harm's way, and threw things at me until I was fully awake.

"To this day, other things still affect me. You know when the garbage truck comes and picks up the bin? That rattling sound? It sounds like anti-aircraft fire to me. That noise still sends me into a state of panic—sometimes when I hear that noise I dive to the ground and cover my head.

"So what I am trying to tell you is that the Vietnam War is not over. Why? Because not a day goes by that I don't think about what happened back there. And as you now know it affects me to this very day. Yeah, as I said before in that video, a lot of Vietnamese died. But I also lost a lot of brothers too. I was lucky. I made it back home. But there isn't a day that goes by that I don't think of them and the sacrifice they made for this country. Sometimes when I sit down and have a beer, watching a game on TV, I wish they could be here with me, just enjoying the simple things in life that many of us take for granted."

Patrick stopped. He was wiping tears from his cheeks. Then he finally took one last look at his notes, looked up to me, and simply stated, "That's all."

A deadly silence saturated the classroom as Patrick concluded and walked back to his desk. The hush was pierced only by sniffles and a whispered "Oh, my God." I looked around to see some students dabbing their eyes, visibly crying; some were staring intensely at the ceiling, valiantly trying not to cry; and a couple of students had their heads on their desks covered by their arms, trying to protect themselves from the heartfelt bomb that just detonated in front of them.

SHATTERING THE ICONS

With class dismissed, Patrick lingered. I knew he wanted to talk. He grasped my hand firmly and with red-rimmed eyes, choked out these words, "Thank you, Mr. Luna. Thank you for giving me time to tell my story. Now, maybe some of these kids will know what war is like and what I and many of my brothers went through."

For Patrick, allowing him to tell of his experience in Vietnam was cathartic. I knew he had a fantastic story to tell, and even though it took some effort on my part, it was worth it. For me, it was one of my best semesters as an instructor. I accomplished what I sought to do. I had presented to the class two sides of the Vietnam experience. A blatantly anti-American video was contrasted by a veteran who had a very personal and decidedly different side of that war. I had effectively presented two sides of the very controversial Vietnam War to the class. I was happy. I had done my job.

****

So if used judiciously, some students can enhance the classroom experience beyond what many instructors can provide. Nevertheless, there is the other side—some students who make an instructor's life miserable and make the learning experience even more difficult. Ironically, technology, touted by many to enhance the learning experience, has in many ways altered it negatively as the following pages will testify. In addition, the intrusion of students bringing their own personal problems into the classroom can also be detrimental to education. But as the following pages will attest, they also have their humorous elements as well.

CHAPTER 16

Judy's Blues: "I Don't Have the Time to Work in Your Class, But You *Still* Have to Pass Me, Mr. Luna!"

Ideally, every student who crosses that threshold into a college classroom should be motivated to learn. Nevertheless, as we have seen in our examination of Marxism, we live not in an ideal world. And although I try as best I can to motivate and inspire students, I have come to the conclusion that some students cannot be compelled to learn even with my most focused effort.

A poignant example of this happened a few years back when I was teaching a US Colonial History class in a large auditorium at the new Clovis Community College. I normally do not like teaching in such a large forum, but I was assigned that classroom, and there was no other room available, so I did the best I could.

About one month before the end of the eighteen week semester, Judy approached me before class. I knew her because she usually sat in the front; but she had a spotty attendance record and would usually leave during the break in the three-hour class. She also had the lowest test scores in the class; nevertheless, I was still willing to help her in the limited time left in the semester. She began her lament, "Mr. Luna, I am failing your class as you know. And the reason is that I cannot see the board."

"You sit in the front. How can you not see the board?" I replied.

"It's just too far away, and I cannot see it."

"Why are you telling me this *now*? We are fourteen weeks into the semester! Why didn't you tell me this at the beginning of the semester?" I pleaded.

"Well, most of the time, I had to leave early for work, and I just didn't have time to tell you."

"You could have e-mailed me."

"I don't have time to e-mail you."

"Why didn't you go to the Disabled Student Services. They can contact me, and then we can make some accommodation for you."

"I don't have time to go to the DSPS office."

"Oh well, OK, if you cannot see the board, I can have someone take notes for you, and then you can study off their notes."

"I don't have time to study someone else's notes."

"OK, then why don't you do what some other students do. You can record the lecture and then play it back at your convenience."

"I don't have time to listen to your lecture."

"You don't have time to listen to my lecture? I know a lot of students are pressed for time. But you can record it and listen to it on your commute to work or school or whenever you are driving."

"I don't have time for that." Judy glared at me.

"OK, then why don't you do an extra credit project? You can do a ten-minute presentation to the class on your term paper. That can give you some extra points."

"I don't have time to do an extra credit project."

At that point, my blood pressure was rising and thoughts of a new career flashed through my head, "Is Home Depot hiring? Maybe I should e-mail my resume to Starbucks tomorrow."

Exasperated, I pleaded, "*Well then, what do you want me to do, Judy?*"

"I want you to *help* me, Mr. Luna," Judy tersely replied.

"But you dismiss every solution I give you."

"I just don't have time for those things."

"If you don't have time for this class, then how do you expect to pass?"

"I don't know. But you still need to *help* me."

"*How do you want me to help you? Do you want me take the tests for you?*" I yelled.

"You still need to help me, Mr. Luna," She declared.

The standoff continued, but the lecture room was filling with students, and I had to stop momentarily. Fortunate for Judy because I was on the verge of violence, I managed to decompress and form these words, "Look, class is starting in a few minutes. Why don't you see me after class, and we can try and find a solution."

"OK."

Judy sat down for the lecture, but true to her form during the break, she left and never returned—not that night and not for the remainder of the semester. I was compelled to flunk her. That was all I could do.

Fortunately, most students are not like Judy. Most students who attend class regularly do give an effort to pass the class. Nevertheless, distractions in the classroom can try even the patience of Job and be a difficult task for any instructor.

CHAPTER 17
The Forgettable Instructor: I Remember Pete, but Pete Doesn't Remember Me

Pete was a student of mine at the Madera Center. From the first day, I knew he was an oddity. Sitting in front, he caught my attention about ten minutes into the lecture when I noticed Pete grab the front of his tank top and began chewing on it methodically like a famished dog working on a bone. Immediately, I thought, "Wow, I haven't seen *that* before." Little did I know what was to come. For when Pete sat in my class that one fateful semester in Madera, Pandora's Box was opened, and all the ills of his persona were going to be spewed upon me.

Thankfully, his mother was there to meet me after the first session. Grim-faced, Pete's mother approached me tentatively. From her countenance, it was evident she was carrying her burdens in life overtly; the principle of which was the realization that her son would never be independent, so she would have to support Pete for the rest of her life. Pete's mom bore that burden continuously with a perpetually disdainful and melancholic look throughout the semester. I never saw her smile.

Pete's mom was a small and frail woman, emaciated by the physical and emotional strains of caring for her son. Apparently too busy or unmindful to do the laundry, her clothing was usually stained with food or soda, the latter of which came from Pete. Her hair was straight, short, and black, the front of which was cut in a bowl-style straight-across-the-forehead clip, which was a practical cut, but it gave her the appearance of an overgrown child. That accompanied by a slow southern drawl and perpetual grimace as she spoke exhibited the demeanor of a person irrevocably overwhelmed by her circumstances in life.

"Mr. Luna, Pete suffers from mild retardation. But he really likes history, and he wants to stay in your class," Pete's mom drawled.

"Sure, I will do what I can. Is he in contact with the Disabled Students Office?"

"Yes, but also, you need to be patient with him. He does some quirky things like chew on his clothes."

"Yes, I know. That's OK. It doesn't bother me."

"Well, I am glad you can help us. I am working two jobs, and I don't have anywhere to put him. He seems to like school, but he is having trouble passing his classes. And I am a single mother. Pete's father is in Lompoc State Prison, and he won't be getting out for another five years."

As she spoke, Pete's mom did not look me in the eyes. With her arms crossed in a defensive manner and head tilting as if on a swivel, her roving gaze examined the walls behind me—the ceiling and the floor, but her distraught eyes never met mine. As Pete's Mom spoke, she reminded me of the sorrow-laden photographs of Dorothea Lange, who chronicled the migrant Okies from the Great Depression, newly-arrived in California and vanquished and desperately clinging to anyone or anything that would rescue them from oblivion. No one smiled in Lange's photographs and neither did Pete's mom.

"I will do what I can to help the both of you," I replied.

SHATTERING THE ICONS

****

Pete attended every class, but he soon became a social pariah among his classmates. He always wore a tank top tattered at the shoulders due to his incessant mastication and carried a Super Big Gulp container full of soda that he sipped and spilled continuously on himself with appalling regularity despite my admonitions to him that drinks were not allowed in class. He carried a massive spine-bending belly that was also frequently invasive. Pete's rotund face was continually blotched by a shotgun-blast of pimples in various states of maturation, some just beginning to bud red on his face and others fully-developed and dotted white, ready for discharge—all fueled by his incessant intake of sugar-laden soda. Pete could not close his mouth completely due to his two protruding front teeth that extended to his lower lip; in sum, he looked like an obese pockmarked rabbit. Crowning his face were large 1950s-style black-rimmed eyeglasses with bottom-of-the-Coke-bottle thick lenses that accentuated his pronounced pimple procurement and also magnified his vacant black eyes. Pete also stuttered, which was the *coup de grâce* to his social ostracism.

Despite Pete's presence, I attempted to conduct my class like any other. On the second day, I engaged the students in a discussion on Reconstruction after the Civil War and asked a general question to the assembled.

"OK, what were some of the problems encountered by the African-Americans after the Civil War ended?"

Pete raised his hand in front of my face, and feeling sympathy for the untouchable, I called on him.

"Well, Mr.-Mr.-Mr. Lu-Lu-Luna, Lincoln was sh-sh-shot," Pete stammered.

"That is right, Pete. Lincoln's assassination really was a blow for black civil rights during Reconstruction, good job."

Pete beamed with his correct answer; he looked like he had just won a multimillion dollar lottery. That was probably the first time an instructor had called upon Pete in class, and the first time he had been given a verbal accolade as well. But then Pandora's Box was opened. Because every time I asked a question to the class, Pete was right there in the front row, squirming in his chair with one hand jutting into the air in front of my face and the other with a vice-like grip on his industrial-sized soda, begging to be called upon again. Pete craved so much for an affirmation that many times, he didn't even wait for me to ask a question to the class, he would just interrupt me in the middle of a lecture.

"So during the First World War, new weapons were used like—"

"OH-OH, MR. LU-LU-LUNA!" Pete shouted with his arm jettisoning into the air like a Nazi salute, "They used machine guns, right?"

"Yes, Pete, they used machine guns. And the other weapons used were—"

"OH, MR.-MR.-MR. LU-LU-LUNA, they-they-they used ga-ga-ga-gas, right?"

"Yes, Pete, gas as well."

"And-and-and-they used artillery, right?"

"Yes."

As I stoked Pete's ego, I took a quick glance around the classroom and saw the majority of the class shaking their heads or rolling their eyes. Pete felt like student *numero uno,* but I was rapidly losing the rest of the flock. Pete and I were spiraling into a universe of our own and if I did not extricate us right away, then I was never going to get through my material.

"Pete, I appreciate your input, but you have to let me get through my lecture, OK?"

Pete's beaming demeanor drained from his face as quickly as if I had told him the winning lottery numbers he held were fake. Pete's head dropped, and he replied meekly, "OK."

Despite my public castigation, Pete continued to interrupt me and cause other problems in class. One public rebuke was not enough to curb his indiscretions; throughout the semester, I had to verbally reprimand Pete continuously to stop his intrusions so I could continue my work. On top of that, other acts of Pete's impetuosity drove me to dash for my bottle of Jack Daniels as soon as I opened my front door.

For example, on my syllabi, marked in bold, were the dates of each of my exams for the entire semester. Rarely did I change them. And when an exam date was approaching, I wrote on the whiteboard in red the date of the exam and the material to be tested in addition to a verbal announcement. Those reminders usually suffice—but not for Pete. On test day when everyone was preparing for the exam, Pete came in, stood before his desk, surveyed the preparatory activity of his fellow classmates, and then turned to ask me meekly, "Mr.-Mr.-Mr. Lu-Lu-Luna, is-is-is there a-a-a test to-today?"

"Yes, Pete, I made the announcement to the class that the exam is today. I also wrote it on the board, and it is also in your syllabus."

"Oh." With his left hand, Pete twisted the top of his tank top in preparation for a chew.

"Well-well-well, Mr.-Mr.-Mr. Lu-Lu-Luna, I-I-I don't have a-a-a Sca-Sca-Scantron," Pete whined to me as he began to ruminate again.

To avoid having Pete go to the bookstore and spend God knows how much valuable test time to purchase an answer sheet, I asked the class mercifully, "Does anyone have an extra Scantron they can spare?"

Thankfully, a kind student came to the rescue with an extra test sheet, and he handed it to Pete.

But Pete was not yet done in disrupting the class in a way that only he could do.

Pete lowered his head and looked up at me guiltily with his opaque black eyes through his grease-stained eyeglasses and sighed audibly, "But-but-but, Mr.-Mr.-Mr. Lu-Lu-Lu-Luna, I-I-I don't have a pencil."

In order to maintain my sanity, I tried to briefly envision my Valhalla—an everlasting stream of ice-cold Heineken beer flowing from a spigot into my mouth. But then I was jolted back to reality. That was the Madera Center, not Valhalla. And Pete still had a problem that needed to be solved.

"Does anyone have an extra pencil?"

Thankfully, another Good Samaritan emerged and produced a pencil for Pete. Finally, he could take the exam.

Exam day was stressful for students, and Pete's forgetfulness was only making things worse for everyone. So when Pete finally sat down and was ready to take his exam, I crouched down, faced him eye-to-smudged-eyeglasses, and articulated very slowly but sternly, "Pete, next time be prepared for the exam."

"Yes, Mr.-Mr.-Mr. Lu-Lu-Luna," Pete replied.

Despite my careful and patient instruction when the next exam came a few weeks later, it was *déjà vu* all over again.

After that, I toyed with the idea of just getting an extra Scantron and a pencil and giving it to Pete on exam day. But I decided not to do it. I wanted him to learn. I wanted Pete to be able to function in the classroom at least on a rudimentary level like being equipped to take the exam on the assigned date.

But apparently, I was asking too much of Pete. The exam charade repeated an additional three times for the remainder of the semester. That reoccurring melodrama was painful enough—but Pete was not yet finished tormenting his instructor. He possessed other idiosyncrasies that occurred throughout the semester with taxing consistency.

Almost like clockwork, after about thirty minutes of lecture, Pete bolted upright from his chair as if he had just been given a jolt of electricity. His chair scraped across the floor noisily as he sprang upright, and Pete gave me a look of pleading pain from his pressured bladder as if in mid-lecture I could miraculously relieve him of his overload. Realizing that I could not help him, Pete staggered to the exit with one hand on his crotch and the other holding his ubiquitous Super Big Gulp, inevitably spilling some of his drink in his calamitous exodus to the bathroom.

After about a five-minute respite without Pete, there he came again, entering the classroom from the rear. But Pete was always sitting in the front, so he had to make his way forward, bumping into desks and students and spilling more soda in his return to his seat. And as the sideshow played itself out multiple times throughout the three-hour class session and the semester and Pete settled in front of me again with the self-satisfied countenance of an empty bladder and mind, at one point I had a sudden epiphany. If there was a God, he was not deserving of my worship. Any deity that allowed this vacuous creature to live and yet take the life of John Lennon was not a being worthy of my adoration.

A Divine plan or not, Pete continued to attend class regularly; despite his attendance, he still did not have the capacity to succeed. And God knows I tried to help him. I gave Pete one-on-one tutorial sessions after class, I e-mailed the lecture notes to his mother so that she could print them and give to Pete to digest slowly, I gave Pete extra time to finish his exams, and I encouraged him to do an extra credit project. I did everything to help him pass the class, but he could not do it. His multiple-choice scores were abysmal; his exam essays were too short and incoherent; his term paper was a disaster; and he refused to do any extra credit.

The ending of the semester came and I was tallying the points for the class, and I come to Pete's scores. I knew what was coming, but I could not ignore it any longer. A quick glance at his overall scores and it confirmed what I had suspected, but I deliberately avoided it for the entire semester: Pete was not going to pass the class.

I was on the horns of a dilemma because in talking to Pete's mom during the semester, she told me that Pete really liked my class, but if he did not pass my class, could he take it over again?

So I contemplated my options, none of them palatable. Would I do the honest thing and flunk Pete and hoped to the fates that he wouldn't end up in my class again like a reoccurring nightmare? Equally important, did I have the patience to handle him again for an entire semester? And even if I did have the patience, did he have the capacity to pass the course legitimately? Or did I just pass him and wash him out of my hair forever? It was Friday, and I had the weekend to consider my situation; semester grades had to be submitted by Monday at noon.

Over the weekend, I faced the obvious. Despite my efforts, Pete was a failure in my class. He could not retain enough knowledge to pass the course. Hell, he could not even remember to bring a Scantron and pencil on exam day. On top of that, his continuous disruptions impeded my teaching, making the entire class suffer as well. But it was not Pete's fault—my constant admonitions fell on deaf ears. I had long since learned to deal with deliberate disruptions by students. But Pete fell into a different category. Pete didn't try to disrupt my class intentionally. Pete just did not have the self-awareness to realize the consequences of his actions. The bottom line was that *Pete did not belong in college.* And Pete's mother knew that as well.

Pete's mother was a polite and kind woman and clearly loved and cared for her son, but she just had too much on her plate: two jobs, an incarcerated husband, and a mentally-challenged son. So Pete's mom did what she thought was necessary. She was using the

Madera Center as a babysitter for him. She had nowhere else to put Pete. She obviously could not afford any specialized daycare, so she just dumped Pete off at the Madera Center before work in the morning where he could be in a safe environment, leave him there, and pick him up at the end of the day. She was secure in the thought that she did not have to worry about Pete getting lost or going hungry.

Was Pete going to enrich his mind in his semesters at the Madera Center? No. Was Pete going to become financially independent after his time at the Madera Center? Probably not. Was Pete going to become a contributing member of society after his term at the Madera Center? Also probably in the negative. The bottom line was that Pete's mom was using taxpayer money to babysit her son, and he was occupying a seat in college that could have been filled by someone else, someone who could put their education to more productive use. It was a flagrant misuse of taxpayer dollars. Pete's mom was abusing the system for her own personal convenience, and that angered me initially.

Nevertheless upon further contemplation, my anger subsided. The intellectually-challenged like Pete posed a unique problem for parents, instructors, and colleges alike. The fundamental question was whether or not individuals of Pete's capacity should even be allowed to enroll at a community college which was theoretically open to all. That was a vexing problem that the case of Pete illustrated clearly. For administrators, Pete was just another student, another number to be tabulated whose expense could be charged to the taxpayers of California. But was his expenditure to the taxpayers worth it? I was the one who had to deal with Pete in the classroom and in essence, played the role of a professional babysitter while simultaneously trying to run a productive class.

Nevertheless, I then recalled Pete's mother's forlorn look as I met her for the first time as she explained Pete's situation to me when she could not even look me in the eye. She knew that Pete didn't belong there. She knew that she was unloading Pete on me, the Madera Center, and on the taxpayers of California. I realized her avoidance in looking me in the eyes was ultimately one of guilt. But in retrospect, considering the many burdens that she had to carry, the nadir of which was Pete himself, my anger diminished.

After a weekend of introspection, I did what I ultimately had to do. I flunked Pete and hoped for the best. Meaning, I hoped he would not appear on my roll sheet for the next semester. I waited with the nervousness of an expectant father until the next semester's roll sheet appeared. The first thing I did was to scan the list for Pete's name. It wasn't there. Pandora's Box was closed once again. I had been redeemed.

****

It was one year later when I ran into Pete again as he was exiting the computer lab in the Madera Center library. He still looked the same, wearing his teeth-tattered tank top and carrying his ubiquitous soda. After a one-year hiatus, I was happy to see him and find out how he and his mom were faring.

"Hey, Pete, how are you doing?" I exclaimed.

Pete merely looked at me through those vacant black eyes and perpetually smudged glasses and waddled past me without a hint of recognition.

I was shocked. I had spent many hours dealing with Pete's special needs. I tried everything in my expertise to help him learn something in the classroom. I tried to deal with his numerous disruptions. And ultimately, nothing worked. I could not even get Pete to remember to bring his answer sheet and pencil to class on test day. So he failed. And I had failed. After all my work and the turmoil he put me and my class through, *at the very least*, I wanted him to remember me. It was all for naught. Pete had already forgotten me.

CHAPTER 18

From Gangsta with a Glock to Guru: The Story of Raj

As noted above, a big demographic changed recently in the population of my hometown Kerman and other parts of the San Joaquin valley is the influx of Sikhs from India. The Sikh population is growing so significantly that in Kerman and neighboring communities, temples have been erected to accommodate that population.

Enter Raj, a recent Sikh immigrant from India. Raj came from a rural and tradition-bound area of India where arranged marriages were still the norm. Raj's parents had recently migrated to America but hoped that their son could maintain elements of his traditional Indian culture. Raj's parents owned some land and a small store near Tranquillity, another small hamlet near Kerman. Raj was enrolled in my Modern US History course when I was teaching at West Hills College in Firebaugh.

Tall and lanky with enormous eyes and an aquiline nose to match, Raj would probably not make the cover of *Gentleman's Quarterly*, but he was amiable, gregarious, and approachable. And although English was not his first language, he tried to adapt to American culture as many immigrants did. But it was not easy. Like many of the newly-arrived, Raj was caught between two cultures. I learned of that predicament on the first day of the semester after the class had been dismissed. Raj approached me and quickly enlightened me of his views.

"Mr. Luna, you should see my family's uncles in India and here in America. They are whack! They never cut their hair! They got long and stringy hair they wrap around their turban." Raj demonstrated as he circled the top of his head with his long fingers.

"It's nasty! And they never shave. I got an uncle with a beard, and after he eats, he's gotta pick the food out of his face. I can't stand that shit, see what I'm sayin'?"

Raj concluded that traditional Sikh culture was not for him. Shorn of his hair and beard, Raj also distained Sikh traditional garb and adopted a mode of dress that he hoped would make him more popular with the girls. And it worked for a while.

Raj usually strutted into class with the customary attire of the hip-hop generation, and I could usually tell Raj was coming even before he entered the room. His music was turned up so loud I could hear his MP3 earphones blasting rap as he approached the classroom from the hallway. And he had the bling too, two large faux diamond-studded earrings, four gaudy gold rings on each hand, New York Yankees baseball cap turned at a jaunty angle from his bobbing head, and thick gold-braided necklaces dangling from his neck. And he usually wore a sagging empire-waist faded blue jeans that barely clung to his thin hips which exposed his underwear to the world.

He talked freely with me and most of his classmates, interjecting his speech with the vernacular of the ghetto world to show his cultural adoption to the hip-hop culture. And for the most part, Raj fitted in. Most of Raj's classmates at West Hills College were Mexican-American wannabe gang bangers who admired the Indian's attempt at coolness. And although Raj was only about a C student, he displayed at least a rudimentary interest in class by showing up for every session and participating in class discussions.

SHATTERING THE ICONS

****

All was well until halfway through the semester. Raj began to show up late for class, which he never did previously. I always made it a point to my students that I did not tolerate tardiness if it became a habit because it caused a disruption, the experience of Pete noteworthy in my mind. And so after a few sessions of Raj coming in exceedingly late, I asked him to stay after class to discuss the matter.

"What's going on, Raj? You are normally on time for class. You need to be here when the class begins because it is becoming a disturbance."

"I'm sorry, Mr. Luna, but I'm late because my license has been temporarily suspended because of my speeding tickets, and so, I have to wait for a ride to class."

"You can't stay under the speed limit coming to class?" I quipped.

Despite my oratorical skills, Raj was not breaking the speed limit to hear my lectures. Raj was a busy man in other ways. Raj was dating an Indian girl from the neighboring town of San Joaquin, but she was enrolled at the University of California at Davis, a considerable distance from her paramour. Besides his courses, Raj was also working on the family farm; consequently, the only time he had to see her was on Friday night. By Saturday afternoon, he had to be back working at the ranch. She was also busy and couldn't drive to Tranquillity, so the only time they could find time for each other was on Friday night through Saturday morning.

So after a week of carnal separation, Raj's ardor piqued. On Friday afternoon, he would jump into his gangster-approved ride, a BMW, flatten the accelerator and race north on Interstate 5 to UC Davis, ignoring speed limits on the way. That was astounding to me. Because without any impediments, the normal speed limit on Interstate 5 was seventy miles per hour. Apparently, that was too slow for Raj.

"So how many tickets you got, Raj?" I asked tentatively.

"I've gotten three in the last month, Mr. Luna. The last one I had to go before the court, see what I'm sayin' because they said it wasn't just speeding, but they wanted to nail me for reckless driving. So my license was suspended, and my parents took my Beemer away."

"Really? How fast were you going?"

"Well, on this last one they got me on the radar at 115."

"What? Were you really going 115?"

"No, their radar must be whack, see what I'm sayin', Mr. Luna, because I swear I was only going 100."

"Only?"

"Well, it wasn't just the speed. I was kind of in a hurry, so I was in the fast lane, but the cars were going too slow *even there*, so I started to pass cars on the right side, see what I'm sayin'? And when I got blocked on all the lanes, I started passing cars on the *right shoulder*—they were just goin' *too damn slow*, see what I'm sayin'? So that caught the attention of the cops, and they wrote me up for speedin' *and* reckless driving, see what I'm sayin', teach?"

"Wow, so what are you going to do?"

"Well, after I pay these fines and get my car back, I'm going to get a new radar detector for my Beemer because the one my cuz installed in my car isn't working, see what I'm sayin'? I want my money back from that ho because I had *no* warning about that last cop. I had *no idea* where he came from. I was jamming near Patterson listening to Eminem when BAM! I look in the rear view mirror, and I see these blue and red lights *poppin,'* and I thought about just sayin,' 'Fuck it' and flooring it to see if those cops could catch up with my Beemer, because it is *juiced*, see what I'm sayin,' but I decided with those airplanes the CHP uses I couldn't get away, so I gave up and pulled over.

"And the cop was *pissed*, Mr. Luna. He said I coulda killed innocent people with the way I was drivin'. Hell, I'm a good driver. Look at all these tickets I got and not one wreck, see what I'm sayin'? Yeah, I drive kinda fast, but I got no time to see my girlfriend, teach. So I *gotta* make up for lost time."

By then, Raj was working himself into a lather, bending over my desk with his bulging eyes, shaking his head, and slapping his right hand into the palm of his left in front of my face like an impassioned defense lawyer trying to save his client from an impending execution. Raj continued, "Well, this cop didn't understand *my situation*. He had all my previous tickets on his computer and called me a 'repeat offender' and shit like that, see what I'm sayin'? So I was gonna diss him, but then he started talking about taking my Beemer away so I thought, 'I need my ride, so don't push it.' But he was *still hot* and that is when he told me he got me on the radar at 115 mph. But I kept my cool after he threatened to take away my ride, see what I'm sayin'? But I swear I was only goin' 100."

"I hope you learned your lesson, Raj," I sighed after that soliloquy.

"Yes, Mr. Luna. But I am still *kinda* screwed. The cops didn't take away my ride but my parents did."

For a couple of weeks, there were no incidents with Raj. Then one day, he showed up late again. Grim-faced throughout the lecture, Raj waited until the class had emptied and then he approached me with the countenance of a sinful Catholic who was about to enter the confessional for the first time in decades.

"I-I-I did a bad thing, Mr. Luna," Raj stammered and blinked his enormous orbs rapidly. I was worried; he was beginning to sound like Pete.

"What's going on, Raj?"

"Well, you know my girlfriend who is going to school at Davis?"

"Yes."

"She's got three brothers, and someone told them we were dating, so they called me and told me to stop seein' her. They are Hindu, see what I'm sayin', and they wanted me to stay away from her 'cause I'm Sikh. They also said that she is a virgin, and that they wanted her to stay that way until she gets married, so they told me to stop seein' her."

I nodded my head. Raj was wringing his hands together in a worrisome manner, but then his disposition changed to an aggressive defense lawyer again.

"So *I got pissed* and told them that *she wasn't a virgin. I was already having sex with her*, that is why I'm going up to Davis every Friday," Raj spewed.

"Oh, my God! Well, how did you get up there in the first place? I thought your parents had confiscated your car?"

"Yeah, I still don't have my license, but I was givin' my parents *so much shit* that they finally threw the car keys at me and said if I wanted to kill myself speeding, then go ahead," Raj exclaimed.

"Anyway, last Friday I was at her apartment, and while we were having sex, I took a picture of us with my phone and sent the picture to one of her brothers to prove that she wasn't a virgin."

"You did what?"

"Well, I wanted to prove to them that she wasn't a virgin anymore, and I thought that was the best way to show them, see what I'm sayin', Mr. Luna?"

"Uh-huh, what possessed you to do something as stupid as that, Raj?" I pleaded.

"Well-well-well, like I said, Mr. Luna, I think I made a mistake." Raj's hand-wringing and rapid eye-blinking had returned.

"Because right after I sent that picture, one of her brothers called me back and said *they were going to kill me*. They were talking about payback and karma and all that shit. I don't believe in karma because I'm Sikh, but it's got me worried." Raj was whispering and looking at me like a guilty dog that had just been caught tearing up the couch.

"Raj, what are you going to do?" I sighed. I was getting a massive migraine by then.

"I-I don't know, Mr. Luna," Raj stammered again.

The next week, Raj came into class with bruises on his face.

"What happened to you?" I said after class.

"Her brothers showed up at my house, called me outside, and beat me up. They told me again that they are going to kill me. I'm scared." Raj was ominously emulating Pete's mannerisms again, that time chewing nervously on his fingernails like Pete did to his tank top.

"You should go to the police," I counseled.

"They won't do anything Mr. Luna. They don't like me anyway with all my speeding tickets, and they also think I'm a gang banger. They are not going to help me."

After a couple of sessions, Raj approached me again after class and gingerly pulled a receipt from his wallet.

"Mr. Luna, I bought a gun," Raj whispered. Raj's eyes grew even larger than usual as he produced the evidence to me from his wallet.

"You must be joking."

"Look, I bought a gun."

Raj then carefully unfolded a piece of paper in the same reverential manner a museum curator would handle the Magna Carta and showed me a receipt for a 750-dollar Glock automatic pistol he had purchased the previous week.

"Are you insane, Raj? Are you really going to use this?" I pleaded.

"I got to protect myself, see what I'm sayin', Mr. Luna? They beat me up and threatened to kill me again."

"I know. But do you really think they are serious?"

"Yeah, they say I ruined their sister for life, see what I'm sayin'? They said she was a virgin and that I took something from her that she could never get again."

"Oh, my God. What does your girlfriend say about all this?" The sudden throbbing pain in the left side of my head signaled that my migraine had returned with a vengeance.

"Well, she's no longer my girlfriend. She broke up with me after I took that photo of us having sex. She said I disrespected her. The ho won't even talk to me, see what I'm sayin'? Every time I call her, she doesn't answer. I've called her at least *twenty times* since I took that photo. I wanted her to help me after her brothers beat me up. But she doesn't answer the phone or my texts. I messed up, Mr. Luna. For all I know, she wants me dead too."

There were only four weeks remaining in the semester after Raj showed me his Glock receipt. The gun was for Raj's protection, but it was also intended to give him a piece of mind—it did not give him the latter. Raj attended until the last week before the final exam, but he was never the same. The happy, gregarious, and laughing Raj was a shadow of his former self. He shuffled into the classroom like the walking dead. His MP3 player was gone—no longer did I hear gangsta music blasting from the hallway as he approached the room. Life was just too somber for Raj to enjoy music. He sat in the corner in the back of the classroom, oblivious to my lectures. He no longer took notes; he no longer participated in discussions--he didn't even look at me. He sat immobile with his arms and legs crossed and stared unblinkingly with his enormous eyes at a vacant spot on the floor just past his feet. An expression of uncalculating doom permeated his face. Raj the litigator had become Raj the condemned man, strapped to the electric chair and waiting for the switch to be thrown—the verdict was guilty.

Raj still wore the bling, but when the reality of all that was glorified in the gang culture came back to hit him in the face (i.e., settling disputes by the fist or gun and the demeaning of women), then his personality changed completely. Raj had deflowered his Hindu girlfriend, and for her family, there was no way to compensate for that crime except by a severe beating or even at the price of Raj's life. In their mind, Raj's transgression was exceedingly grave, so the penance exacted needed to be high as well. On top of that, he flaunted it by taking a photo of himself and his girlfriend *in flagrante delicto* and then sent it through the phone was the ultimate act of disrespect to herself, her brothers, and her family.

****

With two weeks remaining in the semester, Raj was gone. I inquired about his absence to his classmates, but no one had heard anything from him. I also talked to his other instructors who said that he had similarly disappeared. I feared the worst.

For the next month, I actually looked at the obituary columns for his name. Thankfully, Raj was not there. But after a couple of months, I had heard from a student that Raj had been sent back to India by his parents permanently, presumably to save his life. There, Raj could live in his sequestered and traditional village again and probably through an arrangement, marry a traditional Sikh girl and settle down and be a traditional Sikh man. I'm sure Raj's bling, Beemer, and Glock are similarly gone. I wonder if Raj is now growing his hair long and wearing the turban he so distained while in America. Perhaps, it was for the best. American freedom was just too dangerous for Raj.

Chapter 19
Be Chary of Chatting with Your Chonies Down: The Trials and Tribulations of Technology

Five minutes after I told him not to do it, he does it again. We are in a cramped portable classroom at the old Clovis Center Campus. Fifty seats are occupied by fifty students. The one small window at the rear of the classroom is steaming up from the cluster of students and the frigid temperatures outside in a Wednesday night class. I hardly have room to lecture. The first row of seats are about two feet from the lectern, which in turn is the same distance from the whiteboard. I am not claustrophobic, but this is a very tight environment in which to teach. It is a decidedly different environment from the large lecture hall noted above. But since I have no choice in the matter, I try to conduct class as best I can.

The one advantage in teaching in such close quarters is that I can see what students are doing. From that proximity, I can see that the targeted student is not paying attention to my lecture. The offender is easy to spot. He is sitting in the middle but is only about fifteen feet from me. He is easy to spot with the telltale signs of one who is texting, head down as if in meditative prayer and one hand on his lap. I knew that he is engaged in activity that I had explicitly banned at the beginning of the semester.

I stop the lecture.

"Didn't I just tell you to put your phone away?"

The student is so absorbed with his phone that he continues to work his fingers, oblivious to the fact that the lecture has ceased and I am addressing him directly. After a few seconds of penetrating silence, he becomes cognizant of the atmosphere and looks up from his lap into my unblinking stare.

"Oh, sorry about that."

He puts his phone in the front pocket of his jeans and picks up his pen to write notes again. Temporarily satisfied, I continue the lecture, but I am keeping one eye on the transgressor for any reoccurrence of the banned activity.

Sure enough, my suspicions are not unfounded because one minute later, I see that he is not focusing on what I am saying as he initiates his surreptitious activity once again. As if on a greased chair, he slowly slides down horizontally to access his phone more easily. In an attempt to avoid detection, he remains motionless for a few seconds; he then slowly slips his right hand into his front pocket and delicately pulls out his phone and places it on his lap. He waits momentarily, and then, he is at it again because he has reverted to his previous behavior of staring at his lap, right-hand digits rapidly moving, and now, I have had enough.

"DIDN'T I TELL YOU TO STOP TEXTING!?"

This time, my bellicosity catches his immediate attention.

"Oh, sorry about that," he sheepishly admits again.

We are back to square one. I have to put an end to this right now or else the same scenario is going to play out again.

"Get out."

"What?"

"I said leave."

"You are kicking me out?"

"Yes."

A look of undiluted incredulity mixed with embarrassment transforms his countenance.

"I promise I won't do it again," he pleads.

"I said leave."

The student slowly gathers his possessions for his departure. He is tarrying in the hope that I might have a change of heart and allow him to stay. But I cannot. To rescind my own order now would negate any authority I have in the classroom.

All other activity has ceased. Most students have locked their wide-eyed gaze on me. The atmosphere is not unlike I had just divulged to the students that I have terminal cancer and only one month to live.

Finally realizing that I was not going to rescind my order, the student slowly gathers his materials, puts them in his backpack, rises, and meanders his way to the rear of the classroom and out the door to his temporary banishment.

"All right, let us continue then, OK?"

One week later, the offender returns to his original seat. For the remainder of the semester, not once do I see him reach for his phone. Nor do I see any other student reach for their phone either. I have regained control of the classroom. For the rest of the semester, I don't have any further problems with students and their phones.

****

Walking to class at the new Clovis Community College Center I enter the massive open computer lab in AV-1. Winding my way past the banks of computer terminals, I glance at student activity. Typically, only about twenty percent on any given day are actually doing work related to their class. The majority are on social media (e.g., Facebook, Instagram, YouTube, or gaming). Some are multi-tasking—chatting on Facebook while also texting on their phones.

While engaged in these tasks, some are laughing and actively engaging their neighbors. Others are solitary and completely immersed as they sit in front of their terminal. With headphones on, they sit unblinking and almost immobile, oblivious to the world beyond their orbit of activity. These are the hardcore people, and when weaned temporarily from their addiction, they usually run in like-minded packs.

They are easily identified. Mostly male, they usually wear black T-shirts depicted with gothic graphics or other types of funereal clothing. Their hair is long and uncombed, along with two to three days of beard stubble. Due to a lack of sunlight, their skin is sallow with almost a cadaverousness of complexion, and many are obese because the balance of their physical activity is limited to their digits working their phones or computer's mouse. Their addiction to technology has consumed them, and it shows.

Not wanting to sound like a Luddite, I acknowledge that technology does have a place in the classroom. Properly used and balanced with lectures, it can be a useful tool. Additionally, administrators of colleges and universities continuously advocate the incorporation of technology into classrooms for educational purposes, mainly because sources can now be found online that were previously inaccessible. So it would appear that the availability of technology in the classroom advances education inherently. Granted, the technological explosion that has permeated into the classroom and by extension into our everyday lives has allowed us to access information readily, but this accessibility to technology has produced an unintended negative effect.

Maturing in a time when advanced technological access was in its rudimentary state, devices such as smartphones did not exist; yet I can see now how many who did grow up in this digital age are as attached to such instruments as an embryo is attached to the umbilical cord. Smartphones are convenient. They provide us with apps that were unimaginable just a few years ago. But in many respects, technology and smartphones in particular have made communication more impersonal.

For example, one of my former students informed me of the manner in which her boyfriend of many years and father of her child terminated their relationship. Having accepted his marriage proposal, she was in a state of bliss as she spent many weeks in planning their wedding. Then one night at approximately 10:00 p.m., she was in a drive-thru waiting for her food order when she received a short text from her ex-fiancé: "The wedding is off. I have found someone else. Sorry☹."

To her, to be summarily dumped in this off-handed manner was the most infuriating of all. Weeks later when she recounted the event to me, she was still spewing venom, "After all the years we have spent together, raising our child, and he didn't even have the balls to break up with me face to face."

Another problem connected to the advancement of technology is what I term the short-attention span syndrome. Despite the advantages of multitasking, the negative byproduct of this is that students can no longer stay focused on a single task especially in terms of doing research and developing critical thinking skills.

For example, one requirement of my class is a research paper. The assignment is not difficult; it merely calls for the student to choose a topic on some historical event within the timeframe of the course and to produce a minimum six-page typed paper. Then I allow the students to submit a rough draft so that I may be able to give a preliminary critique and the paper can be revised as per my instructions.

So during a Modern US History class, one of my students, Jason, approached me and told me he wanted to do a paper on the Watergate affair. I was pleased; I surmised that Jason would have no trouble finding resources on one of the most significant presidential scandals of the Twentieth Century. I gave my approval and wished him well.

"I also want to submit a rough draft and have you look at it as well," Jason said.

"I look forward to reading it," I replied.

Approximately three weeks later, I agreed to meet Jason after class. He told me he had a copy of his rough draft for me to critique.

Jason approached me after class with his draft. He had a grim look on his face.

"Mr. Luna, here is my rough draft. I only have two and a half pages for you to look at though. I might have chosen the wrong topic. There are hardly any sources on Watergate."

"What?" I replied. "What sources did you look at?"

"Well, I 'Googled' Watergate and checked the first ten websites. They all repeat the same thing. As I said, there is just not enough information on Watergate, so I should choose a different topic, right?"

I was dumbstruck. Watergate was a monumental United States historical event, and Jason was going to throw in the towel because he could not find more that two and a half pages of information.

"OK, you 'Googled' it and hit a roadblock. Did you try books?"

"No, I didn't check."

Quickly off the top of my head, I enumerated books I have already read concerning the Watergate Affair. "There is *All the President's Men*, by Bob Woodward and Carl Bernstein, *The Right and the Power* by Leon Jaworski, *Blind Ambition* by John Dean, *To Set the Record Straight* by John Sirica, *Witness to Power* by John Ehrlichman, *The Ends of Power* by H. R. Haldeman, and *The Whole Truth* by Sam Ervin, Jr."

Jason gave me a deer-caught-in-the-headlights look. "You mean I have to *read* a book?"

Jason's lament is not unusual in today's academic world. The focus needed to read a book is becoming a rare discipline in today's technologically charged world. We are so attached to technology. Whether it be our phones or a laptop, the digital world has impeded our ability to focus on a single task. Technology and more specifically the internet, more often than not function to fuel our short-attention span tendencies. Like a baby entranced by the dangling of multiple car key chains, our addiction to technology impedes our ability to concentrate on a single task. And unfortunately, this lack of focus extends to instructors as well. When proctoring an exam, I always bring a book with me to read.

One time, the night manager at the Clovis Community College came by and saw me open a tome as the exam began.

"So you are a reader?" She raised her eyebrows in amazement. I was appalled. I merely nodded my head in agreement, but internally, I was ready to exclaim, "Shouldn't all instructors be readers?"

Another poignant example of this is perhaps the most important book ever written—the Bible.

When I am teaching a World Civilizations course and the time comes to cover Christianity, I usually ask this question.

"OK, how many in this class are Christian?"

Typically at least ninety percent raise their hands.

"Now, keep your hands up. From those with raised hands, how many of you have read the Bible— not just a few Gospels—but the *entire* book?"

All hands fall from the air, accompanied by sheepish looks.

"Well, don't you think you should read it? If you believe the Bible is the Word of God, and your eternal fate is dependent upon that word, don't you think you should read it?

Then I drop the bombshell.

"I am not a Christian. But I have read the Bible—*twice*. Don't you think you Christians should do it at least once?"

Murmurs ensue throughout the class. Someone usually replies, "Mr. Luna, why aren't you a Christian?"

I want to reply, "Because I read your Bible," but I usually hold my tongue from this retort.

But of course who has the focus to read the entire Book of Books? There are few who have the discipline to do it. Because there is Facebook, and this deity is not some remote being, this deity must be supplicated continuously.

Of course, Facebook has its advantages. With Facebook, I can keep in touch with family and friends in ways I could not before. But it can also be an unholy addiction. One of my Facebook friends finally closed her account permanently. I asked her why, and she recounted her epiphany that finally severed her yolk to Facebook.

"You know what I call Facebook? I call it Facecrack," she confessed to me like a repentant alcoholic at an AA meeting.

"Let me tell you what happened to me once when I was using my laptop at home, Frank. Facebook is that insatiable urge to post a picture or make a statement on your wall and expect a 'like' or 'share' something you found while scrolling and then wait for someone to react. I wait for that little red box on the upper right corner of my laptop to come on. Then I look and see my friends who are also online with their little green lights on, and I wonder why they have not reacted to what I have just posted. Are they connecting with someone else? Are they seeing something more interesting than what I just posted? Why haven't they given me a 'like' yet? I need them to recognize me. See how important my life is. Take a gander at this great party I attended. See how much fun I am having. So why don't you give me a 'like?'

"So I continue to wait for that red box to light up. I can feel my blood pressure rise while I wait for a response... Then it happens. The red box lights up with a '1' in it. I check to make sure they are responding to what I just posted. And if it is, then I am happy.

Someone is noticing what I am doing. I admit it. I get an immediate rush from that. The adrenaline pumps through me, and I get that tingle, that surge of energy. I am somebody because one of my friends gave me a 'like.'

"But it doesn't last. The rush wears off quickly. Hey, those other green lights are still on, what is going on here? I keep waiting for that red box to come on again. But it doesn't. So I need to do something else to get their attention. So it's time to up the ante. Now, I post a short video I have on my laptop to see what kind of response I get. Then it happens again. 'Bam!' instantly I get another '1' in my red box. Wow, I have a smile from ear to ear! I am in heaven again!

"But after a couple of minutes that wears off too, see? I have to do something else. So I check to see who still has their green light on, and I message one of them with 'Hey, what's up?' Then I wait again. My heaven soon turns into hell when I get no response. That means I am not worthy right now of an immediate message response. My friends are engaged in something more important than me. How depressing is that? Don't you understand I need your attention *right now*? So I wait a couple of more minutes. Damn, still no response! My blood pressure is going up again. I need that rush again. So now, I go to the next friend who is online. 'Hey, what's up?' I message. My laptop goes 'Pop!' This time, I get an immediate response. I'm chatting with my friend! How cool is that, right? So we continue messaging and then 'pop,' the person I first messaged has just contacted me. Whoa! I am way too popular now. I am a celebrity. I am chatting with two people simultaneously. The adrenaline is surging through my veins, and I am in nirvana again.

"Now, a different call arrives, the call of nature. But I cannot disconnect now. If I disconnect now, then I will lose my simultaneous chats and my instant celebrity status. So I have to improvise. Plan A, where is my smartphone? I can conveniently continue my chats with that. I give a quick glance around the living room but it is nowhere to be found. And I cannot hold it long enough to do a thorough search around my house. No phone? No problem. Plan B, I unplug my laptop. With my wireless internet, I can continue chatting in the bathroom while I do my business. So I run to the bathroom with my laptop in tow, place it on the floor in front of the toilet, drop my chonies, grab my laptop again, and continue with my chats. I have taken multi-tasking to a new level. I am sitting on the porcelain throne, emptying my bowels, and with my laptop literally on my naked lap, I continue chatting with my two friends.

"I am doing it all when I hear the familiar whistle from my smartphone. Of course, I left it in the bathroom after I took a shower one hour earlier. The whistle is muffled because I left my bath towel on top of it. No wonder I couldn't find it. 'Tweet!' It goes off again. Someone is texting me. Of course I cannot just let it go unanswered. Despite the fact that I am chatting with two people on Facebook, I have to respond to my phone *now*.

"So here is where things literally get messy. Did I tell you I had taken a laxative the previous night? I most certainly did. I had been constipated for a couple of days, so that is why I had to answer the call of nature immediately. Without becoming too graphic, when my phone whistled the second time, I was still in the middle of answering nature's call. So I placed my laptop on the floor in front of the toilet again and then jumped over it to reach my phone. Well, you know how laxatives work, right? Sometimes, you just can't hold it. So when I jumped, that did it. I just literally exploded all over my chonies and all over my laptop. I landed and looked back at the damage. Was it bad? Oh, yeah. Was it disgusting? You bet. My chonies, I only needed to wash. But I had also splattered all over my brand new seven-hundred-dollar laptop. It was ruined. Why was it ruined? Because I couldn't wait. That is how addicted I was to social media—the immediacy of social media. It was controlling my life like a drug. I needed that continuing instantaneous rush of communicating with someone else even though I was already chatting with two people on my laptop. I was living off that rush and dying from it too. That moment was my epiphany. When I looked down and saw my laptop destroyed by my own fecal matter because I couldn't wait, that was it for me. That is when I realized something had to change. I closed my Facebook account forever. And I have not been regretting it one single moment. I am no longer addicted to 'Facecrack.' And I have learned that I don't have to respond immediately to any texts unless it is an emergency. I can accomplish so much more now and not live and die with my cellphone and those damn little red and green lights anymore."

Fortunately, my friend's addiction to social media produced no damage apart from a ruined laptop. Others are not so lucky. Texting while driving has become more hazardous than drinking and driving among teenagers. Recent documentation culled in 2010 and 2011 has noted more than 3,000 teen deaths and 300,000 injuries annually from texting and driving.[219] One local casualty affected me deeply.

****

Tiffany was enrolled in my World Civilizations course at the new Clovis Community College. A woman of about twenty with shoulder-length flaxen hair and flashing cobalt blue eyes, her glowing skin and trim body all flaunted the flush of youth, beauty, and health. Tiffany was intelligent as well, and her interests expanded well beyond her major in civil engineering. Often, she asked insightful and perspicacious questions on historical phenomena well beyond what was expected from a student majoring in another discipline. Her enthusiasm for the course was also reflected in her perfect attendance.

So it caught my attention when about halfway through the semester, Tiffany stopped coming to class. The incident with Raj had already transpired, so naturally, I feared the worst. My foreboding was confirmed one day when I exited class during the last week of the semester.

"Mr. Luna," a weak spectral voice called out from behind me.

I turned around and saw a feeble female limping toward me very slowly.

"Yes?"

"It's me, Tiffany."

The unrecognizable wraith continued its approach.

"Tiffany, from class."

Only from about ten yards did I finally recognize who it was.

"Tiffany, is that you?"

"Yes, I am sorry for missing class, Mr. Luna."

I attempted to cloak my shock but it was impossible for before me stood a battered shell of the young woman I knew previously. Immediately, I recognized that Tiffany's youthful form was forever gone. Her once shiny flaxen hair was matted and frayed; both eyes were red-rimmed, half-lidded and lifeless; her trim and taut body sagged under the weight of physical trauma, augmented by a major impediment in her left leg, which she almost dragged while walking; and her disfigurement was crowned by the incongruity of her skull, the top of which was visibly asymmetrical to her lower half.

"Mr. Luna, I was in an accident. I was driving on Willow Avenue on the way to your class when I almost had a head-on collision."

"How did that happen?" I could only mutter.

"I was driving when a girl going in the opposite direction crossed the center line and clipped me. I saw her coming and leaned on the horn, but I realized that she was distracted and not watching the road. So I swung right to avoid a head-on collision, but it was not enough. She hit me, and I flipped over and totaled my car."

"Oh, my God, how did she wind up in your lane?"

"She was texting and didn't realize where she was going until it was too late."

Tiffany then wheezed a deep breath and listed her maladies.

"I spent about six weeks in the hospital. The doctor said if I wasn't in such good condition, I probably would have died. I fractured my legs, ribs, skull, and jaw. I ruptured my liver and spleen. I was on dialysis due to kidney damage. I cannot see clearly out of both eyes. I sustained a severe concussion, and my memory is impaired. I am not sure I can continue in college because I cannot retain any information. My doctors have told me that I will never fully recover, and I will continue to need many years of physical therapy. But I am lucky. At least I am alive."

Tiffany then approached me closely and feebly shook my hand.

"Thanks for your class. It was very interesting. You are an excellent instructor."

I opened my mouth in response but could not emit a sound. For one of the few times in my life, I was rendered speechless.

Tiffany turned and then limped down the hallway. I never heard from her again. She withdrew from class and from Clovis Community College as well. A young, vibrant, beautiful, and intelligent young woman was ravaged in the prime of her life because of a texting driver. A driver, compelled to respond immediately to a text, lost control of her car, and in a split second altered her and Tiffany's life forever. I was depressed for the remainder of the semester.

PART IV
Afterthoughts

CHAPTER 20

Picking Up the Pieces: Reflections on the Shattered Icons

Looking back to when I labored on Abuelita's farm, my political evolution took a long time and a tremendous amount of soul-searching to reach its present state. As noted above, it was a painful experience because what I investigated and learned took me on a divergent path from what my family, media, and academics told me what was correct. But as I explored further and finally severed my Marxist moorings, it ultimately was something I had to do. For my own peace of mind and ultimately respect for the evidence I uncovered, my transformation had to take place.

I included my experiences on Abuelita's farm primarily so that the reader may know my childhood was not an easy one. In fact in terms of labor, it was comparable to what the farmworkers experienced. That was why I could identify and sympathize with their toil. And not surprisingly, I initially assumed that institutions like the UFW as endorsed by most academics and the media were there to defend and protect the farmworker. Nevertheless, as we have seen, the UFW has failed. Similarly with Marxist states, their professed egalitarianism is also counter to the needs of the worker.

Despite the ample amount of evidence to the contrary and the dissemination of conservative media, the vast majority of Marxist pontificators in this country still stick to their guns. For the Marxist academic, capitalism is evil because it inherently produces economic stratification. So their knee-jerk reaction is any political system or group that promotes an egalitarian model must be good, right? Because these academics envision capitalism as inherently evil, any step toward the eradication of that inequality must be seen as *good* and *for the people*. But as noted in the previous chapters, a thorough examination of the evidence has disclosed that these societies and systems have not in fact helped the poor or the oppressed but in fact have been agencies of further oppression. The attempts to collectivize societies have not alleviated inequality but in fact have exacerbated it. But the Marxist academic turns a blind eye to this reality. One hundred million dead at the hands of Communist societies has nary raised an eyebrow from the academic Left. At best, they acknowledge that *mistakes* have been made at the hand of Marxist societies. Consequently, a sober reckoning and critique of these societies itself remains to be made by those who advocate it.

Advocating socialist principles while immersed in a capitalist nation compels the Marxist academic to assume a duplicitous position. They present evidence to highlight the inequalities of capitalism as noted in the physical toll of the domestic servants in Beth's class: lower back pain, varicose veins, and ankle and foot problems. Beth highlighted this demeaning labor as worthy of our castigation when it takes place in a capitalist society while the exceedingly more oppressive and punishing physical labor in the Soviet gulag, China, Cambodia, and Cuba are ignored or dismissed because this labor is perceived as contributing to the Revolution.

And to these instructors, the Revolution is all that matters. Any critique of the Marxist model is squelched as noted in Beth's class by Steve's attempt to question it. That confrontation piqued my interest and inspired me to investigate on my own the points he raised in the classroom. And as noted, the defense of Marxism takes more subtle forms as when instructor Bob only allowed presentations that critiqued capitalist systems. In that class also, no dissent was allowed. In those and other classes I took at Fresno State, no inquiry was raised or allowed by any Marxist instructor as to whether these so-called egalitarian systems implemented to extinguish the inherent inequality of capitalism might in fact bring forth a new inequality. No inquiry is raised or allowed by any Marxist instructor as to whether the only people who truly benefitted are the revolutionary leaders who implemented and enforced these systems. No inquiry is raised or allowed by any Marxist instructor as to when or how the "state will wither away" and we will all live in a utopia free from inequality, strife, and war. No inquiry is raised or allowed by any Marxist instructor as to the fact that on some level, there is some benefit to capitalism. No inquiry is raised or allowed by any Marxist instructor as to the real possibility that Marxist ideology itself might be flawed. No, enraptured by their egalitarian blueprint, the Marxist instructor myopically fords ahead, pontificating to the class, "this is science" or "this is the solution" without addressing any of the above-mentioned queries.

And of course, this kowtowing applies to Cesar Chavez and the UFW, who have been virtually canonized by the Leftist academic community. Chavez has been deified in many ways, most notably locally with his pantheon statue on the Fresno State campus. Like collectivist societies, the sanitized version of Chavez and the UFW is presented to the students. And most media follow it without abatement. In the classroom, rarely is the story continued when Chavez moved his organization to La Paz and sequestered himself and his high-ranking lieutenants from the very people they were supposed to represent. Nor is there any inquiry into the accounts of the UFW beating and assaulting undocumented workers on the Arizona-Mexico border. Nor is there any inquiry in re the millions of dollars of unaccounted funds. Nor is there any inquiry that the money received by the UFW are not dispersed to the workers but like Fresno

State, are rather mostly used in an iconographic sense: the naming of schools, roads and the like to prop up the image of Chavez only, not to benefit the farmworker. In sum, there is no inquiry allowed to the proposal that the UFW is actually harmful to the farmworkers.

No, in the classroom, we are indoctrinated to believe the UFW represents the farmworker. They have only their best interests in mind, so don't critique the union. Because if one critiques the union, it is tantamount to critiquing the farmworker themselves. The Left-leaning academic will not concede that the UFW has lost its way and has only the propagation of its iconic image as an advocate of the farmworker in mind. But as we have seen, to rebuke the UFW or Marxism is not allowed. Like Marxism, the Leftist academic cannot allow any denunciation of the UFW because once again, to allow it is heresy. Any reprimand of these organizations triggers an immediate backlash along with the attendant name-calling, "You are a cocoa-nut," "you are a *vendido*," "you are a Republican" or going back to my Abuelita's castigation upon me, "*cola prieta*." To these goose-stepping academics and apparatchiks, the iconography of these institutions must be sustained at all costs, lest they lose faith in the cause. It is the image that counts, not the reality.

****

As we have seen, America's tolerance for dissent—especially in the media and academic communities—has provided the instructor in the classroom with a forceful pulpit in which to vent their spleen. Yet to remain credible, I call upon the Marxist academic, comfortably established in a capitalist environment to at least give acknowledgement of a system and a country that allows for such dissent. Perhaps this is asking too much.

Failing that, I call upon the Marxist academic community to practice what they preach. If they do not acknowledge the system that economically supports them and provides them with a forum for objection, at least by their lifestyle, show us the way. Illuminate a shining path toward the socialist future.

Discard your bourgeois trappings and live the life your prophet, Karl Marx commanded. Dissolve your marriages; sell your private property; do not subject others to wage slavery; and finally, when you have freed yourselves of these bourgeois trappings, move into a commune. Show us, by your actions and lifestyle, that the Marxist way is the better way. By doing this, the Marxist academic would at least gain some respect in my eyes. But do not continue live the very lifestyle you condemn in the classroom. Do not proudly proclaim, "I am a Marxist" and continue to live the bourgeois lifestyle so vilified by Marx. This is one of the tremendous hypocrisies I see in the American Marxist academic community today.

Coming to terms with and acknowledging the benefits of teaching in this country is a critical step in the proper direction as it pertains to the Marxist academic. The Marxist pontificator can deliver from his bully pulpit a stream of denunciations against the United States and its oppressive capitalism and not fear any significant repercussions. As we have seen, for many academics, it is even lucrative to denounce the United States and its practices. To these individuals, I propose a scenario: if the tables were turned and an academic teaching in a Marxist country would choose in their classroom or writings to denounce the country that supported them, what would be the reaction from that government? Would they be given financial support? Would a Marxist government tolerate their denunciations? Of course not. As we have seen, if the dissenting academic were in the Soviet Union, China, Cambodia, or Cuba for example, they would no doubt find themselves with a bullet to the head or on a one-way ticket to a labor camp for *reeducation*.

As noted above, the Marxist academic in this country is engaged in a game of tremendous hypocrisy. While they insist on academic freedom in the classroom to teach whatever they want, no matter how corrosive it is to the very system that supports them, and expect no repercussions therein, they in turn suppress any opposition to their point of view, while simultaneously promoting their institutions as centers of *diversity*. A reckoning is needed. The proliferation of technology, which theoretically should give students ample ammunition to challenge their professors, has actually produced the opposite effect. Addicted to the immediacy of social media, gaming, and cell phones, student's attention span has been altered. The siren call for the immediate and new technological stimulation beckons the student into a short-attention span mindset. The focus and discipline needed in reading a book and remaining trained upon on a single task so that that information can be analyzed effectively has almost become a lost skill among students. Critical thinking skills, the very skills that the academic world is trying to promote through the use of technology, has in many ways become a force working against it.

Imagining myself as a student in today's technologically saturated world, I am not sure if I would have had the discipline to focus and analyze what I witnessed in Bob's and Beth's class, and the subsequent drive to meticulously research and critique their teaching methodology utilizing the stacks of books in the Henry Madden library. Perhaps, I would have just swallowed their indoctrination as fact. Fortunately, I did not. But I suspect that most students today with their truncated attention spans do not have the honed critical thinking skills needed to refute this form of indoctrination. Consequently, the academic community must reassess the excessive utilization of technology in the classroom. A more balanced approach using less technologically based material in the classroom is needed to wean students from their reliance on technology and steer them to more traditional sources to cultivate and hone their critical thinking skills more effectively.

Additionally, the Leftist academic community must reassert its position vis-à-vis the society which gives it legitimacy and stature. The Marxist academic, working and *profiting* in a capitalist world, must come to terms with their own ideology and cease the indoctrination that permeates their classroom. Their first step is to acknowledge that Marxism is not a science but is in fact merely an interpretation of events or historical phenomena. Secondly, the Marxist academic must come to terms with their demonization of capitalism and also acknowledge that the United States, with all its inherent problems, has in the past and still does presently have the capacity to self-correct the ills that plague it. Thirdly, by ceasing their tactics of indoctrination, they should encourage and allow different point of views in part by utilizing students' perspectives as I did in the case with Bob and Patrick. The Marxist academic must respect their institutions' stated goals of encouraging diversity by presenting historical phenomena in the most neutral way possible. Only in this way can true diversity thrive in the classroom. Only in this way can the classroom become what it is ideally promoted to do—to become an environment where all points of dissent and discussion are allowed without having an academic tell you what is right and what is wrong. Only through this process can true diversity occur in the classroom—and not indoctrination—as is currently happening.

End Notes

1. Horowitz and Laksin, *One-Party Classroom*: 6
2. Rollins: 6
3. Ibid: 55
4. Ibid: 63
5. Ibid: 147
6. Ibid: 158
7. Ibid: 171
8. Ibid: 129
9. Solzhenitsyn, *The Gulag 2*: 10
10. Johnson, *Modern Times*: 70
11. quoted in Ibid: 70
12. Salisbury: 565
13. Johnson, *Modern Times*, 69
14. Werth, "A State against Its People," in Courtois, et al. *The Black Book of Communism*: 78
15. Solzhenitsyn, *The Gulag 1*: 10
16. Ibid: 93
17. Leggett: 197-198
18. Solzhenitsyn, *The Gulag 1*: 445
19. Ibid: 60-61
20. Ibid: 88

21. Johnson, *Modern Times*: 269
22. quoted in Conquest, *Harvest of Sorrow*: 226
23. Solzhenitsyn, *The Gulag 1*: 76
24. Solzhenitsyn, *The Gulag 2*: 49
25. Ibid: 87
26. Ibid: 89
27. Ibid: 126-127
28. Solomon: 119
29. Ibid: 138
30. Ibid: 177
31. Solzhenitsyn, *The Gulag 2*: 99
32. Ibid: 109
33. Ibid: 128
34. Ibid: 390
35. Solzhenitsyn, *The Gulag 1*: 435
36. Werth: 114
37. Solzhenitsyn, *The Gulag 2*: 126
38. quoted in Werth: 124
39. quoted in Mitrany: 60
40. Furet: 141
41. quoted in Mitrany: 81
42. quoted in Johnson, *Modern Times*: 270-271
43. Conquest, *Harvest of Sorrow*: 4
44. Ibid: 75
45. quoted in Conquest, *Harvest of Sorrow*: 118
46. Grossman: 157
47. Kravchenko: 119
48. Conquest, *Harvest of Sorrow*: 231
49. quoted in Ibid: 233
50. Grossman: 157
51. Conquest, *Harvest of Sorrow*: 287
52. quoted in Ibid: 257

53. Ibid: 182
54. Johnson, *Modern Times*: 270
55. Werth: 167
56. Conquest, *Harvest of Sorrow*: 301
57. Chang and Halliday: 25, 49.
58. Ibid: 322
59. Ibid: 464
60. quoted in Chang and Halliday: 282
61. Becker, J.: *Hungry Ghosts*: 34
62. Chang and Halliday: 328
63. Labin: 148
64. Chang and Halliday: 546
65. Ibid: 436
66. Labin: 353
67. Chang and Halliday: 325
68. Ibid: 429
69. Becker, J.:188
70. Labin: 349
71. Ibid: 314
72. Becker, J.: 189-190
73. Chang and Halliday: 430
74. Becker, J.: 50
75. Ibid: 52
76. quoted in Chang and Halliday: 439
77. Labin: 97
78. quoted in Chang and Halliday: 439
79. Ibid: 438
80. Ibid: 626
81. quoted in Johnson, *Modern Times*: 654-655
82. Ibid: 655
83. Kiernan: 49
84. Johnson, *Modern Times*: 656

85. Kiernan: 167
86. Ibid: 83
87. Becker, E., *When the War Was Over*: 258
88. Kiernan: 204
89. Johnson, *Modern Times*: 656
90. Stuart-Fox and Ung: 79
91. Kiernan: 421
92. DePaul: 70
93. Johnson, *Modern Times*: 656
94. Becker, E.: 235
95. Ibid: 282
96. quoted in Ponchaud: 66
97. Becker, E.: 259
98. Johnson, *Modern Times*: 657
99. quoted in E. Becker: 316
100. Thomas: 808
101. Ibid: 808
102. quoted in Ibid: 819
103. Ibid: 835, 838
104. quoted in Ibid: 880
105. quoted in Hollander, *Political Pilgrims*: 63
106. quoted in Fontova: xix
107. Thomas: 919
108. Ibid: 953-954
109. Ibid: 954-955
110. Paterson: 99
111. Thomas: 974
112. Ibid: 985
113. Ibid: 1019
114. Ibid: 1074
115. quoted in Fontova: 70
116. quoted in Thomas: 1077

117. Ibid: 1085
118. Ibid: 1233
119. Ibid: 1239
120. Hollander, *Political Pilgrims*: 259
121. quoted in Ibid: 261
122. Valladares: 358
123. Fontova: xx
124. Thomas: 1258
125. Paterson: 258
126. Thomas: 1289
127. quoted in Ibid: 1290
128. Ibid: 1297
129. Johnson, *Modern Times*: 624
130. Fontova: xx
131. Ibid: 2
132. Johnson, *Modern Times*: 627
133. Courtois: 4
134. Daly: A5
135. O'Brien: A18
136. Ferris and Sandoval: 28
137. Ibid: 69
138. Ibid: 86
139. Ibid: 93
140. Dunne: 25
141. Ferris and Sandoval: 138
142. Ibid: 144-145
143. Garcia: 110-111
144. Ferris and Sandoval: 210
145. Ibid: 113
146. Ibid: 117
147. Dunne: 26
148. Ibid: 26

149. Ferris and Sandoval: 140, 172
150. Ibid: 218
151. Ibid: 244
152. Garcia: 180
153. quoted in Ibid: 190
154. Ferris and Sandoval: 226
155. Ibid: 229
156. quoted in Ferris and Sandoval: 227
157. Garcia: 143
158. Wozniacka: A9
159. quoted in Griswold: B7
160. quoted in Ibid: B7
161. Pawel: "Chavez Heirs Run Thriving Business as UFW Flounders." A1 and A8
162. Pawel: "Laborers Reap Little as UFW Drifts Away." A10
163. Pawel: "Chavez Heirs Run Thriving Business as UFW Flounders." A8
164. Marx and Engels: 77
165. quoted in Johnson, *Intellectuals*: 79
166. quoted in Hollander, *Political Pilgrims*: 118
167. quoted in Ibid: 122
168. quoted in Ibid: 145-146
169. quoted in Ibid: 170
170. quoted in Horowitz, *Unholy Alliance*: 47
171. Hollander, "Judgements and Misjudgments," in *The Collapse of Communism*: 182-183
172. quoted in Ibid: 184-185
173. quoted in Ibid: 180
174. quoted in Hollander, *Political Pilgrims*: 294
175. quoted in Collier and Horowitz: 31
176. quoted in Ibid: 229
177. quoted in Ibid: 230

178. quoted in Hollander, "Judgements and Misjudgments": 166
179. Collier and Horowitz: 148
180. quoted in Paterson: 233
181. quoted in Johnson, *Modern Times*: 628
182. quoted in Ibid: 628
183. Hollander, *Political Pilgrims*: 243
184. quoted in Fontova: 22
185. quoted in Horowitz, *Unholy Alliance*: 74
186. quoted in Fontova: 123
187. Conquest, *Reflections on a Ravaged Century*: 116
188. quoted in Conquest, *The Harvest of Sorrow*: 151
189. Kopelev: 249
190. Collier and Horowitz: 290
191. Johnson, *Intellectuals*: 60
192. Johnson, *Modern Times*: 52
193. Ibid: 270
194. quoted in Heller and Nekrich: 238-239
195. quoted in Hollander, *Political Pilgrims*: 63
196. Fontova: 24
197. Sanchez: 57-58
198. Ibid: 193-194
199. quoted in Hollander, "Judgements and Misjudgments,": 177
200. see Hersey: 25
201. see Johnson, *Modern Times*: 426
202. see Ibid: 423
203. see Spector: 502
204. see Feifer: 104, 109
205. Ibid: 277
206. see Spurr: 283
207. see Johnson, *Modern Times*: 423-424
208. see Ibid: 424
209. quoted in Feifer: 229

210. see Johnson, *Modern Times*: 425
211. see Feifer: 572
212. quoted in McCollough: 394
213. quoted in Ibid: 442
214. see Johnson, *Modern Times*: 426
215. see Ibid: 426-427
216. quoted in Spector: 543
217. quoted in Ibid: 559
218. see Johnson, *Modern Times*: 425
219. Ricks: A10

Bibliography

Becker, Elizabeth. *When the War Was Over: The Voices of Cambodia's Revolution and Its People*. New York: Simon and Schuster, 1986.

Becker, Jasper. *Hungry Ghosts: Mao's Secret Famine*. New York: The Free Press, 1996.

Chang, June and Jon Halliday. *Mao: The Unknown Story*. New York: Alfred A. Knopf, 2005.

Collier, Peter and David Horowitz. *Destructive Generation: Second Thoughts about the Sixties*. New York: Summit Books, 1989.

Conquest, Robert. *Harvest of Sorrow: Soviet Collectivization and the Terror-Famine*. New York: Oxford University Press, 1986.

———. *Reflections on a Ravaged Century*. New York: W.W. Horton and Company, 2000.

Courtois, Stephane, Nicolas Werth, et al. *The Black Book of Communism: Crimes, Terror, Repression*. Translated by Jonathan Murphy and Mark Kramer. Cambridge: Harvard University Press, 1999.

Daly, Matthew. "Obama Honors Chavez Legacy." *The Fresno Bee*. October 2, 2012, p. A5.

DePaul, Kim, ed. *Children of Cambodia's Killing Fields: Memoirs by Survivors*. New Haven: Yale University Press, 1994.

Dunne, John Gregory. *Delano*. New York: Farrar, Straus & Giroux, 1971.

Feifer, George. *Tennozan: The Battle of Okinawa and the Atomic Bomb*. New York: Ticknor & Fields, 1992.

Ferris, Susan and Richard Sandoval. *The Fight in the Fields: Cesar Chavez and the Farmworkers Movement*. New York: Harcourt Brace & Company, 1977.

Fontova, Humberto. *Exposing the Real Che Guevara: And the Useful Idiots who Idolize Him*. New York: Sentinel Press, 2007.

Furet, Francois. *The Passing of an Illusion: The Idea of Communism in the Twentieth Century*. Translated by Deborah Furet. Chicago: The University of Chicago Press, 1999.

Garcia, Matt. *From the Jaws of Victory: The Triumph and Tragedy of Cesar Chavez and the Farm Worker Movement*. Berkeley: University of California Press, 2012.

Griswold, Lewis. "Workers Rally against UFW." *The Fresno Bee*. September 24, 2013, p. B7.

Grossman, Vasily. *Forever Flowing*. Translated by Thomas P. Whitney. New York: Harper & Row, 1972.

Heller, Mikhail and Aleksandr Nekrich. *Utopia in Power: The History of the Soviet Union from 1917 to the Present*. Translated by Phyllis B. Carlos. New York: Summit Books, 1986.

Hersey, John. *Hiroshima*. New York: Vintage Books, 1989.

Hollander, Paul. "Judgements and Misjudgments," in *The Collapse of Communism*, Lee Edwards, ed. Stanford: Hoover Institution Press, 1999.

_____. *Political Pilgrims: Travels of Western Intellectuals to the Soviet Union, China, and Cuba, 1928-1978*. New York: Oxford University Press, 1981.

Horowitz, David. *Unholy Alliance: Radical Islam and the American Left*. Washington, D.C.: Regnery Publishing, 2004

Horowitz, David and Jacob Laksin. *One Party Classroom: How Radical Professors at America's Top Colleges Indoctrinate Students and Undermine Our Democracy.* New York: Crown Forum, 2009.

Johnson, Paul. *Intellectuals.* Harper and Row, 1988.

_____. *Modern Times: From the Twenties to the Nineties.* New York: HarperCollins, 1991.

Kiernan, Ben. *The Pol Pot Regime: Race, Power, and Genocide in Cambodia under the Khmer Rouge, 1975-79.* New Haven: Yale University Press, 1996.

Kopelev, Lev. *The Education of a True Believer.* Translated by Gary Kern. New York: Harper and Row, 1980.

Kravchenko, Victor. *I Choose Freedom: The Personal and Political Life of a Soviet Official.* New York: Charles Scribner's Sons, 1946.

Labin, Suzanne. *The Anthill: The Human Condition in Communist China.* Translated by Edward Fitzgerald. New York: Frederick A. Praeger, 1960.

Leggett, George. *The Cheka: Lenin's Political Police.* Oxford: Clarendon Press, 1981.

Marx, Karl and Frederick Engels. *The Communist Manifesto: A Modern Edition.* New York: Verso, 1998.

McCollough, David. *Truman.* New York: Simon & Schuster, 1992.

Mitrany, David. *Marx against the Peasant: A Study in Dogmatism.* Chapel Hill: The University of North Carolina Press, 1951.

O'Brien, Matt. "Sainthood Proposed for Farm Labor Leader." *The Fresno Bee.* March 29, 2015, p. A18.

Paterson, Thomas. *Contesting Castro: The United States and the Triumph of the Castro Revolution.* New York: Oxford University Press, 1994.

Pawel, Miriam. "Chavez Heirs Run Thriving Business as UFW Flounders." *The Fresno Bee.* January 21, 2006, p. A1 and A8.

_____. "Laborers Reap Little as UFW Drifts Away." *The Fresno Bee.* January 20, 2006, p. A10.

Ponchaud, Francois. *Cambodia: Year Zero.* Translated by Nancy Amphoux. New York: Holt, Reinhart and Winston, 1977.

Ricks, Delthia. "Alarm Grows Over Texting in Cars." *The Fresno Bee.* May 10, 2013, p. A10.

Rollins, Judith. *Between Women: Domestics and Their Employers.* Philadelphia: Temple University Press, 1985.

Salisbury, Harrison. *Black Night, White Snow: Russia's Revolutions, 1905-1917.* New York: Da Capo Press, 1981.

Sanchez, Juan Reinaldo with Axel Gylden. *The Double Life of Fidel Castro: My 17 Years as Personal Bodyguard to El Lider Maximo.* New York: St. Martin's Press, 2015.

Solomon, Michael. *Magadan.* New York: Vertex Press, 1971.

Solzhenitsyn, Alexander. *The Gulag Archipelago One.* Translated by Thomas P. Whitney. New York: Harper & Row, 1974

_____. *The Gulag Archipelago Two.* Translated by Thomas P. Whitney. New York: Harper & Row, 1975.

Spector, Ronald H. *Eagle against the Sun: The American War with Japan.* New York: The Free Press, 1985.

Spurr, Russell. *A Glorious Way to Die: The Kamikaze Mission of the Battleship* Yamato, *April 1945.* New York: Newmarket Press, 1981.

Stuart-Fox, Martin and Bunheang Ung. *The Murderous Revolution: Life and Death in Pol Pot's Kampuchea.* Sydney: Alternative Publishing Cooperative Limited, 1985.

Thomas, Hugh. *Cuba: The Pursuit of Freedom.* New York: Harper and Row, 1971.

Valladares, Armando. *Against All Hope: The Prison Memoirs of Armando Valladares.* Translated by Andrew Hurley. New York: Alfred A. Knopf, 1986.

Wozniacka, Gosia. "UFW Fights Ebbing Number." *The Fresno Bee.* April 23, 2011, p. A9.

About the Author

Frank M. Luna has taught history at various colleges in the San Joaquin Valley in Central California. He lives in Clovis, California, and is currently working on a book about his travels to Japan. He can be reached at fmluna2000@yahoo.com.

CPSIA information can be obtained at www.ICGtesting.com
Printed in the USA
BVOW08s1043230416

445348BV00001B/71/P